No Pasta? Are You Kidding Me?!?

A True Beginner's Guide to Healthy Cooking With Less Wheat, Sugar & Junk

Diana Marshall

Published by Buy The Book Publishers, Ltd. Inquiries should be
directed c/o 411 N. 6th St. Suite 1081, Emery, SD 57332

ISBN: 0-6922-3712-7
ISBN-13: 978-0-6922-3712-0

"Diana Marshall's book takes the mystery out of healthy eating. She tells of her own experiences and mishaps along the way which makes reading the book so enjoyable. She never preaches but gently points out the mistakes we might be making and how to correct them without upending our whole lives. I've never felt better and have had to buy smaller pants and clothes to fit after all the weight I've lost!"

Diane L., Phoenix AZ

*"One of the best things about **No Pasta?** is that you don't have to run all over town trying to find the ingredients for the recipes. It's healthy eating without driving yourself nuts."*

Lisa G., Forestville, CA

*"After using the tips in **No Pasta?** I was able to experience life without food cravings for the first time ever! It was so amazing to me and has making the transition to healthy eating so much easier."*

Lisa H. Reg. Nurse, Asheville, NC

"As one of Diana Marshall's first students, I can attest to how great her method is. It was a significant turning point for me and made such a difference in my life."

Anne M., Severna Park, MD

Thank You

I have a very special group of friends who have been with me on different parts of this journey and from beginning to end: Vagabundo Diane, Neighbor Sandy, Sister Lisa, Maggie and Marsha, Barbara A., Lisa H., Joan A., the Dog Park Gang - Sandra, Anne, Patience, Jill. I love and thank you all!

My main two mainstays, my compatriots who were with me every step of the way, were Coleen and Julie. They were there to pick me up when I fell down, read through any and all drafts, make meaningful suggestions and generally just be there for me. They are true friends in every sense of the word, and I literally could not have gotten through this without them.

A special thank you to my two angels in heaven: My mom and Dr. Joan Campagna. Dr. Joan helped me get through my various ailments over the years and never laughed too hard when I came up with my various theories about what was wrong with me. She was the epitome of what a kind and caring doctor should be. My mom was a vivacious, spunky woman who never stopped supporting my sister and I in any of our endeavors. She would have gotten a kick out of this one.

Contents

1. In the Beginning..1

2. My Story.. 11

3. I Refuse to Starve! 15

4. Diana's Overview of a Plan for Healthier Eating.................... 17

5. The Not So Good For You Foods.. 25

6. Cravings versus Calories... 33

7. Making Good Choices Is the Key 36

8. Compromises, Setbacks, and Other Issues 39

9. Pump Up the Volume.. 49

10. Why I Am a Flexitarian...51

11. It's Really Not That Complicated 55

12. Exercise 57

13. Keeping the Cooking Simple 59

14. Breakfast : The Most Important (and Problematic)
Meal of the Day 63

15. Mix-and-Match Meal Plans and
the Importance of Leftovers.............................. 66

16. What and Where to Buy 69

17. Recipes 75

    Pomegranate Tea Drink 77

    Basic Berry Smoothie... 80

    Tasty Mixed Vegetables 82

    Super Seeds (and Nuts) 85

    Perfect Rice Every Time...................................... 86

    Super Stock... 89

    Basic Sauces and Gravies 91

    Savory Vegetable Soup 94

    Chicken Quesadilla and Bean Soup 97

    Three-Bean Lentil Soup 99

    Diana's Deviled Egg Spread 101

    Salads and Dressings 103

    Egg Foo Young... 106

Cheesy Brussels Sprouts 108

Steamed Artichokes 110

Vegetable and Potato Frittata..112

Mistaken Identity Mashed Potatoes....................................113

Killer Chicken with Pan Gravy..115

Turkey à la King... 117

Sparkling Shrimp
(or Sparkling Salmon, Swordfish, Sea Bass, or Tilapia) 119

Salmon or Crab Cakes..122

Healthy Beef Stroganoff..124

Stupendous Stir-Fry...126

Amazing Pizza Crust...129

Dreamy Dark Chocolate Sauce...132

Chocolate Frozen Banana Treat 133

Fruit Cobbler 134

18. My Favorite Health and Food Gurus 135

19. This Is Nowhere Near the End...139

Author Biography...141

I
In the Beginning...

~~~~~~~

Actually you could have a little pasta—it just shouldn't have any wheat flour in it. But as a friend of mine of strong Italian heritage announced to me proudly... **"Then It Is Not REAL Pasta!"** I had to admit—he had a point...

Seriously, all you hear about on TV and in the media these days is that everyone needs to "eat healthier." You have heard about the enormous health and weight-loss gains that can come from not eating wheat/gluten, sugar, and processed junk foods. But when you investigate the actual how-to cookbooks, they can seem downright scary. They don't have many of the ingredients you are used to eating and cooking with. And they do have lots of ingredients you've never even heard of and would have no idea where to buy. How do you get started when you don't know where to begin?

This book is written by someone who was absolutely a beginner FOR beginners. Its purpose is to help inform and transition you to healthy eating and cooking in a gentle, "user-friendly" way—one that is not a giant shock to your system. I firmly believe that for some people, if you don't give yourself and your body time to ease into a whole new way of eating, you may suffer from withdrawal, feelings of deprivation, awful nasty cravings—all hardships that may make you give up, think this isn't for you, abandon healthy eating altogether, and go back to the Horrible Processed Foods that are slowly killing you.

I do not think that all the doctors and experts on TV and elsewhere understand how big a barrier this newness, unease, and sense of dread can be to a lot of folks. They advocate "7-Day Detox" and "15 pounds in 15 days" health diets that eliminate virtually every customary food you have ever eaten your entire life. And they don't call them diets—they call them "lifestyle changes." But really, the only lifestyle change that works is one you can stick with. Otherwise, sadly these quick fixes may be more akin to the fad diets of yesteryear—no matter how much they talk about how great "healthy" eating is. Then they present to us these wonderful success stories, people who look great and make noises about how "it wasn't as difficult" as they thought it would be. But do they tell you about all the non-success stories of those who took one look and gave up before even starting? Or the ones who couldn't stick with it over the long haul, and wound up leaving the whole experience feeling worse about themselves than ever before?

We can all guess that eating healthy is better for oneself. *Then why aren't more people doing it?* Because—simply put—the transition can be incredibly difficult. You are after all, largely giving up a way of eating that has been with you your entire life. Please don't misunderstand me: I don't think the hard-core, "cut out all the bad foods in one surgical strike" approach is bad or wrong. It can be a quick ticket out for some personality types. But the goal here is to get healthy—not to prove how masochistic or stoic you can be getting there. I don't think "the just tough it out" approach is the ONLY approach that can work. Only you can decide what works best for you.

I follow most of the experts on most of their rules most of the time.

I have read and listened to almost all the best experts, and I write about the ones who affected me the most in chapter 18, "My Favorite Health and Food Gurus." As you may be well aware, there is no consensus on certain points about recommended healthy eating plans. For example, some experts allow dairy, others don't. Some recommend a higher degree of meat and saturated fats than others. Soy, corn and even eggs are sources of debate. Of course it is confusing. The lack of consensus among top experts can – in and of itself - become an excuse to not get started. After all – if all the experts who know this stuff backwards and forwards can't agree - how can a mere mortal like myself be able to figure it all out?

I knew that same fear and confusion, because it stopped me dead in my tracks on more than a few occasions before I finally took the plunge. The most important thing I have now come to realize is that it takes a combination of "experts" and "real people" to pull off real change. What I wound up doing was taking from all and actually making a synthesis, or potpourri, of all the most common recommendations and then designing a plan and recipes that worked best for **ME**. I incorporated what I could realistically accomplish balanced against their fairly rigorous strictures. That combining of recommendations is what finally worked. Your personality style, family background, and unique habits will hopefully lead you to your own creative, balanced, flexible plan and recipes that will work for **YOU**. That is the point of this whole book.

Who this book is intended for: This book is intended for any person who wants to eat healthier, no matter the reason. Any person who has vague health issues that just never seem to go away, including joint pain, back ache, gastric reflux, mood swings, digestive issues (such as irritable bowel syndrome, or IBS), fatigue, difficulty sleeping, skin problems...any person who is overweight (primarily in the belly) and is unhappy with his or her appearance because of it...any person who has gotten a stern look from a doctor when discussing too-high blood sugar and cholesterol numbers. Better nutrition and a healthy, anti-inflammatory diet will help all these problems—perhaps not solve them, but definitely help. How much is up to you.

Also, this book is intended for people for whom spending a lot of time in the kitchen is not a way of life and might never be. My recipes are generally quick, easy, and very basic with shortcuts and a lot of how-to information. But what I have found is that even serious foodies can be intrigued with the notion of getting unhealthy ingredients out of their recipes and substituting them with simple flavors and combinations of healthy alternatives that might not have occurred to them...yet.

Who this book is NOT for: This is a **GIANT DISCLAIMER**. I am not a doctor or a nutritionist, and I do not have any medical training or scientific expertise. I barely know what the glycemic index really is. If you have been diagnosed with a serious medical condition—such as diabetes, heart disease, and/or an immunological disorder—you need to follow your doctor's or their nutritionist's advice precisely. Also, although I advocate getting rid of some foods as much as you can, nothing in this book is exclusionary of any one food or food group. Therefore, if you have been diagnosed with a food allergy, such as celiac disease (allergy to wheat/gluten), or an allergy to dairy, soy, corn etc. you need to buy a very serious book on how to eliminate those things completely. I advocate not eating wheat (including whole grain) and wheat flour, but some of the prepared foods and sauces I use might have traces of wheat/gluten in them. That darn stuff is now so pervasive in any processed food of any kind, it seems to get in everywhere. I can't even begin to promise that my recipes have avoided everything anyone could be allergic to.

In writing this book, I have tried to keep the science parts to a minimum so as not to overwhelm you with a lot of wonky, data-filled recitations, studies, or footnotes that will make your eyes roll back in your head. Because of this, some of my reasons for recommending or discouraging certain foods may seem like information that is new or unusual to you. If at any time you feel that way, please stop and research the subject matter for yourself on the Internet, and make up your own mind. If it is easier for you to learn things visually, the Dr. Oz website (www.doctoroz.com) has great video information, just plug the topic you are researching into the search box. I absolutely invite and encourage you to "double check" me and learn as much as you can about the whole subject of healthy eating, shopping and cooking. There is a wealth of information out there for you to explore.

There is one bit of science I feel should explain however, because I use the word "inflammation" so often throughout the book. Understanding inflammation is absolutely critical to understanding why so many of us need to change our eating habits.

Inflammation is a major source of pain and chronic illness affecting us today. Much of the inflammation we suffer from comes from the mass produced, processed foods we eat. Because of this, we can make choices every day to help our body be well or unhealthy by what we decide to eat.

Simply put, inflammation is the body's healing response to what it perceives as harmful substances that have entered or injured it. Inflammation is necessary to heal trauma, injury and infections. But things can go terribly wrong when even very low levels of food allergies, intolerances and sensitivities force this very same protector of the internal organs and tissues to get over stimulated and defend against the things you eat as if they were "invaders." Your body keeps trying to attack and repel the bad foods, chemicals and unfamiliar additives, firing up the immune system and creating an inflammatory response. This low-level constant attack by the internal immune system over time becomes unhealthy and aggravates many chronic illnesses and their symptoms - causing pain and sickness that make us feel so miserable. This war inside your body can happen without you even suspecting or knowing the connection between the two, I know I missed it for YEARS!

Adding to the trouble, these immune system responses can aggravate certain diseases (arthritis, psoriasis, IBS to name just a few) which can be diagnosed by a doctor but that are just below the radar screen of his/her being able to tell you what the actual cause is. Any time you hear "We believe part of the cause may be an immune system disorder or response..." then you can be assured that unhealthy foods are inflammation triggers and can aggravate the "flare-ups" that make you feel your worst.

When you combine the inflammatory effects of an unhealthy diet with the hormonal imbalances that are caused by being even moderately overweight or obese and toss in a sedentary lifestyle, you have a perfect stew of unhealthiness that does not allow you to live your fullest, best life possible.

Well... that certainly **was** me!

Before

Before

Now

2
My Story

I had never really thought of myself as "obese." I am 5'4" and wavered around 175 and 185 pounds for more years than I care to count. But I told myself "I carried it well" and didn't look "fat." You know, all the little lies we tell ourselves so we can continue to eat bread, pizza, deli meat sandwiches, ice cream, **pasta**—all that stuff we know in our hearts would be so difficult to give up. But, in fact, the lies were getting harder and harder to tell myself.

I was a size 16/18 and was verging on size 20—a line I did not want to cross. Also, XL was starting to turn into 2XL—HORRORS! All my clothes were fitting uncomfortably, and my belly would just not stop protruding. I was doing all the things we "almost" fat women do to hide our status—wearing lots of black clothing, holding our purses in front of us, using jackets and vests to cover up our waistlines...many of you are familiar with the whole range of visual tricks we have to try to minimize our reality. But the inescapable truth was that I was desperately unhappy with my appearance. I was also bloated, fatigued and felt defeated.

But even all that was not enough to make me change. What finally drove me to desperation was **PAIN**. Yes, old-fashioned, garden-variety chronic back pain. I'll spare you the gory details, but when I was about forty-eight, I suffered a crippling neurological condition called transverse myelitis from which I somewhat recovered, but it left me with a limp and uneven walking gait. From that I developed arthritis in my back and hips. I was always sore and, with any sort of extended activity—walking, sitting, or standing—my spine and joints would become aggravated and inflamed and the pain unbearable. Eventually it almost stopped me from doing what few outdoor activities I could enjoy. Yours may be golf, tennis, walking, or playing with your kids. Once your pain or your weight makes you start backing away from an active lifestyle, it's really downhill from there.

I knew instinctively that losing weight would probably help my pain by taking pressure off my joints—but what I didn't know was how much of our diet, what we eat, can trigger or lessen **inflammation** (see previous chapter) which is the true source of pain. I saw Dr. V. J. Vad (see "My Favorite Health and Food Gurus," Chapter 18) on a PBS special, and it changed my life. He brought home to me how very much I could change my situation with nature's greatest creations for us humans—nutritious, real food.

I started with meats and significantly reduced eating meats with inflammatory omega-6 fatty acids (chicken, beef, and pork). That helped. The next thing staring me in the face was sugar—with the help of raw, organic bees' honey in VERY reduced amounts, I got a handle on the soda problem. I lost some weight, and I was beginning to feel better. But nothing shook my world like getting **wheat** out of my life!

I had been contemplating giving up wheat for some time, but frankly, I was so afraid. My whole life I had been such a bread and pasta junkie. I was at a local health food store and saw some garlic millet and flax, gluten/wheat-free crackers. They had so much garlic they actually burned spicy hot in my mouth. I loved them! I thought to myself, maybe, just maybe, if I had something like this to help me through, I would finally have the courage to do what I needed to do. About that same time I saw Dr. William Davis (author of *Wheat Belly*) give a presentation, I read his book, did the research and I became determined to just say NO to wheat. It wasn't easy and I talk about wheat withdrawal in Chapter 5. But I did it. The rest, as they say, is history!

About a month or two later, my clothes started feeling MUCH looser. I actually had to go out and buy some new pants. I don't weigh myself, so I have no idea of the speed at which I lost pounds, but people started remarking that I looked like I had lost weight. The first I really noticed it was when I went to a family reunion three months later and didn't feel the need to Photoshop myself out of the family photos.

But the main miracle was that I was not in as much pain. I didn't have to take the next day off to recuperate after a day of some outdoor activity. My need for pain medication lessened tremendously. I felt like I could exercise moderately again, which was a bonus that I'm sure contributed to my overall wellness. My blood pressure came down, and the rest of my glucose and cholesterol numbers finally came down to within normal ranges. My complexion glowed and looked younger, my energy blossomed, I was sleeping sounder, and **I just felt so much better!**

In short, all the promises of the advocates of getting wheat out of my life had come true. I have always been a "the proof is in the pudding" kind of a gal, so the fact that this change in eating habits had actually delivered—when ALL the other multitude of diets I had been on over the years had failed—was a revelation.

I have lost at least three dress sizes and about forty pounds. And two years later, I have kept it off. And, just as importantly, I feel no desire to backslide. Seriously, a big serving of pasta now just looks like joint pain and yellow belly fat on a plate and has no appeal for me whatsoever—which is an amazing change from a few years ago.

Any time you have a significant weight loss, your friends notice and ask you how you did it. Some are even actually interested. For those who were—I told them. They were absolutely horrified at the thought of giving up commercial breads, most packaged baked goods, wheat flour **pasta** (hence the title of this book!), and refined or artificial sugar. But after giving it some thought, the friends who were truly craving change came back to me, asked questions and were intrigued. I began to show them some of the drinks, meals, and desserts that I had invented and how I cooked them. They saw they actually wouldn't have to be THAT deprived. The ones who started making similar changes, or started inventing their own recipes, started losing weight too. I even began giving some informal cooking classes in my apartment. Friends asked me to write my recipes down...

...and that was the start of this book! I wrote this book for one reason and one reason only—to explain how I got healthy and lost weight and to help other people who want to do it too. If they like this book and it helps them, then maybe they will recommend it to their friends, and so on and so on. I don't need a giant marketing campaign, and I don't care if I don't sell a million copies. I don't intend to create a cooking empire and wind up on the Food Network. If you ever need help with any of the how-to aspects of this book, please don't hesitate to e-mail me at:

nopasta@outlook.com.

I will do the best I can to help. If you don't mind, I may use your question anonymously on a blog I write—to help other folks and share information. Just think of us as a bunch of girlfriends, sittin' around a digital kitchen table swapping tips and talking about diets, health, and weight loss!

3
I Refuse to Starve!

~~~~~~~

For me, pain was the final straw that made me desperate enough to commit to serious change. It may well be an entirely different motivator driving you to healthier eating. For example, getting a diagnosis of being "pre-diabetic" can be very scary. But for all of us, having come to the "aha" moment of clarity that all the processed foods, sodas, and sugars that we are eating are making us overweight and sick, the harder question then becomes—**How** do we change?

Most women work outside the home or are incredibly busy in the home. If eating healthier means special trips to the health food store buying exotic foods they've never heard of that are too expensive—or involves cooking that is overly complicated—it probably won't happen and will be put off for another day. Another day of boxed mashed potatoes, Lean Cuisine–type frozen food, too much meat, fried food, and, worst of all, diet sodas or sugary fruit juices and yogurts.

Also, no one wants to go hungry—ever. Especially me! When I tried conventional diets, even healthy ones, I always wound up feeling hungry and tired—a total recipe for disaster. Frankly, I was scared to death of the severity and deprivation I knew I would suffer on most of the heath food diets I had read about. The experts on TV talk about how you do not have to be deprived on their plans, but then they still stick a piece of salmon next to some broccoli without much else and point to a big basket of vegetables as the stuff we can eat as much of as we want. YIKES!

I came to realize that if I was ever to climb up this mountain for good, I needed to design quick, easy recipes for nutritious food that would be tasty and that I could eat a lot of so that I wouldn't be hungry. I needed to design healthy substitutes for the things I enjoyed that were making my life painful. So I set about using my kitchen as a laboratory to design methods of preparing food using healthy (but not exotic) quality (but not expensive) ingredients as simply as possible.

Trust me, there is the other side to any of your food addictions and cravings, but it can be tricky to get there. I like to think that the suggestions and recipes contained in this book could be analogous to a supervised withdrawal from a severe drug addiction. You know... you've seen it in movies and TV shows... "cold turkey," which looks horrific and painful, versus the more gentle approaches, which feature substitute medications to relieve the worst of the symptoms and withdrawal effects. I know which one I'd choose! And I did.

I don't want for you to have to reinvent the wheel. This book is my effort to add to the vast volumes of literature on this very subject but in a way that makes the whole process more digestible (pun intended!). I want to share my methods, tips, and recipes with other folks who are simply desperate to feel better without starving.

4
Diana's Overview of a Plan for Healthier Eating

~~~~~~

Things to Cut Out Almost Completely

Wheat: Please try to cut out all wheat, even "whole-grain wheat." Very renowned nutritionists and doctors are now coming around to the fact that this stuff is nothing but bad news for your health and your waistline (see more on wheat in "The Not So Good For You Foods," Chapter 5). What I can tell you is that this is the ONE single factor that made the most difference in my effort to fight painful inflammation and food cravings. It wasn't until I gave up wheat entirely that I really started losing weight and began to feel better. I feel strongly enough about this subject to challenge you to give up wheat for a period of a month or two and see if you don't feel incredibly better.

Processed Food: You know what this is—almost all the stuff made by Big Food Corporations allegedly for your convenience that comes in boxes, cans, and most frozen meals. Unfortunately, in addition to all the processed junk foods that are easy to identify, the vast majority of allegedly "natural," "healthy," and "gluten-free" products fall into this category as well. They are simply overly processed versions of their toxic cousins (cookies, pasta, granola bars) and contain "junk" carbohydrates and sugars that do you no good as substitutes. They will sabotage your efforts completely in no time. Careful label reading is essential before purchasing any of these products.

There are exceptions; I outline them in Chapter 5.

Sodas and surgery things: My favorite One and Only OK added sweetener—**raw** (<u>unprocessed</u>) **organic bees' honey.** It's not made or processed in a lab, and humans have been digesting this gentle sweetener for centuries. It also contains antioxidants! Try to find local raw honey from local farmers and beekeepers. It can be tough to give up sodas, which is why one of my first recipes was **Pomegranate Tea Drink** (p. 77).

Deep Fat Fried Things: This should go without saying...

Things To Significantly Limit

Meat: Meat should constitute no more than 25% of a meal. **NO processed meats** (i.e., deli sandwich meats or sausages with nitrates). Grass-fed beef, pasture-raised pork, and free-range chickens are the healthiest meats. Factory-farmed animals are housed in unhealthy, unsanitary conditions, and the stuff they are fed is terrible. I only eat meat that I have purchased myself and that has been raised the equivalent of a 4 or 5 on the Whole Foods Meat Rating System www.wholefoodsmarket.com (see Chapter 10). Of course, no antibiotics or added hormones belong in our meat or our dairy cows.

Dairy: I prefer low-fat cheese, sour cream, whipped cream, and mayonnaise, which I've found OK if used in **very small amounts.** Full fat is better than non-fat as they must process the milk too much to get the fat completely out. Your first priority is to find a "milk" that you like that does not come from a cow—i.e., almond or coconut milk—for use in smoothies and sauces. I prefer unsweetened coconut milk, but it really is a matter of individual taste. Greek yogurt is great. Avoid added sugar in any dairy product, which includes almost all yogurts especially those parading around as "good for your tummy." If you need a probiotic, and most people do, find a good supplement.

Corn: Corn and its' by-products are very starchy and most of it is highly genetically modified (GMO). Corn chips (with no oil) are marginally better than pretzels which are a wheat and salt problem. If you are in a Mexican restaurant, corn tortillas are OK, but flour are unacceptable—you get the idea...just stay away from it as much as possible.

Starchy carbs: Try to decrease your portions of all starchy carbohydrates. Of the bunch, I believe whole grain rice is your best carb. If not a fan of brown rice, try jasmine brown rice which doesn't have as much of a "nutty" texture and taste. Mix it half and half with white rice until you can transition. Throw in some beans for extra volume. Definitely limit potatoes which are almost all starch and glucose (sugar). People ask me all the time, "Why rice over potatoes?" Please form a visual of what Asian middle-aged tourists look like coming off a tour bus versus their peers living in the United States and Northern Europe. Get the picture? The damage can occur now and over a lifetime.

Things That Are OK - But Don't Overdo

Eggs: The whites of an egg are high in protein and yolks contain other vital nutrients. If scrambling, using two whites to one yolk is a good ratio. Please buy eggs only from healthier, anti-biotic free, free-range or at least cage-free chickens.

Tropical Fruit: Tropical fruit such as pineapples, mangos, and so forth can be quite high in sugar, so be careful with them.

Soy: The least processed the soy product, the better. Shelled **edamame** (the actual "bean" of the soybean) is a great source of protein and organic tofu is fine. Soy burgers and soybean oil, which are at the other end of the spectrum, are horrid—read the ingredient labels. Watch out for soy products masquerading as something else, for example, soy milk and cheese.

Fish and shellfish: The cold water fishes, particularly salmon, are high in good-for-your-heart omega 3 fatty acids. Do not batter or deep fry. Fish broiled or sautéed with a little low-sodium tamari sauce, spray olive oil, garlic, and lemon is delicious. You should try for wild caught. If you are concerned about possible contaminants in seafood, there is great information on the internet about how often it is safe to eat different kinds of seafood depending on where they swim in what body of water or ocean. If you do not eat seafood at all (and even if you do) please consider a fish oil supplement especially if you have chronic joint pain or want a healthier heart.

Things That Are A-OK

Green Vegetables: Eat green vegetables all you want, raw or cooked with every meal. Try with some lemon, low-sodium tamari sauce (which is aged, generally gluten-free soy sauce), unsalted garlic powder, and, yes, even a little butter! Cook in a garlic vegetable broth for extra flavor. See **Tasty Mixed Vegetables** (p. 82). Save the broth for soup. Colored vegetables are good for you too!

Salads: Of course, salads are the healthy eaters' traditional best friend and for good reason. Sprinkle with **Super Seeds** (p. 85) for extra crunch. I provide recipes for low-cal dressings that actually taste really yummy in my Salads and Dressings recipes (p. 103).

Fruits and Smoothies: The main elements of a healthy breakfast and great as snacks.

Beans: Some people's digestive systems have issues with beans, but if you can tolerate them, they are a great source of protein. Lentil soup is great as a main dish, a snack, and as a sauce/gravy.

Low-sodium broth soups

Snacks That Are OK

Apples: The peel part is better for you (less sugar and more fiber)—the inner part is for horses!

Crackers or chips: Surprisingly, if eaten in moderation, chips are not the worst thing in the world. Consume wheat-free only, nothing fried or covered in oil. Try www.samisbakery.com online for crackers made with millet and flax. Their garlic millet and flax chips are to die for! If not a garlic lover, try the Italian herb flavor. They have a millet and flax cinnamon cracker that can substitute for a cookie when absolutely necessary. Another good brand of chips is Mary's Crackers. But hands down, the best "chip" is thinly sliced heart of cauliflower.

Celery sticks: These are tired but true and, of course, can be enjoyed with a healthy dip.

Dips: Try guacamole, hummus, tzatziki sauce, **Diana's Deviled Egg Spread** (p.101) and fresh salsa.

Egg whites: Hard boil them for salads. Try pickling them in the juice they pickle green olives in for an extra treat.

Frozen bananas: Enjoy with **Dreamy Dark Chocolate Sauce** (p. 132).

A cup of **Savory Vegetable Soup** (p. 94).

Tuna fish or canned sardines: When mixed with celery, green onion, and hard-boiled egg white this can be used as a dip or spread.

Things You Cook With

When it comes to oils, butters, and spreads—the main rule to follow is the least processed the better. Corn, sunflower, and soybean oils are the most overly processed and the highest in inflammatory omega-6 fatty acids, and you want to avoid products if these are in the ingredient labels.

Butter: I have been going back and forth about butter for years. I hardly do any dairy, so I was always on the lookout for healthy vegetable based alternatives. But they had a bunch of inflammatory vegetables oils, which are not good for you. Now that organic butter is widely available and saturated fats aren't thought to be the villains they once were, I have switched back. Remember how good vegetables tasted with a little butter on them when you were a kid? If you can't do dairy at all, try Earth Balance nondairy, nonsoy spread, which comes in a peach-colored container.

Coconut oil: For higher-heat frying (sautéing), this is the best choice. I use it as well in what little baking I do. It does not have a sweet taste, so you can fry your meats and vegetables in it.

Olive oil: Olive oil is the best of the vegetable oils. Use for low- to medium-heat sautéing and salad dressings. I like the olive oils infused with garlic! I keep a bottle of **nonpropellant**, organic olive oil spray around all the time for when I want a light coating to scramble or cook an egg.

Tamari sauce: Tamari is actually old-fashioned soy sauce all dressed up. It is made from the soybean but is aged and has a mellower yet more complex flavor than soy sauce. Please get the organic, low-sodium, gluten-free variety.

The 90/10 Rule

Being good 90 percent of the time is better than being bad 100 percent of the time.

-or-

Don't let the food police get you down

5
The Not So Good For You Foods

~~~~~~

First…the good news! I really don't give a darn about coffee (please use coconut or almond milk and raw honey) or alcohol (in moderation) or dark chocolate (at least 65 % please). All the things you use to get by—just use in moderation, and, as my great friend Jill says, "Seek balance first."

OK, let's get done with the bad news by moving on to the worst of the foods you should not be eating:

Wheat

All things made of wheat should be eliminated as much as possible from your diet, including bread, PASTA, cookies—anything made from wheat flour. **And it doesn't matter if it's "whole grain wheat"**—as far as your body chemistry is concerned, it has the same problems.

Here is a very brief synopsis of what the science surrounding this grain is now showing:

1. The wheat of today is not the same wheat as it was fifty years ago. In the last few decades, food scientists got their hands on wheat and began to modify its DNA in a process that creates what are known as genetically modified organisms (GMOs). They did this in order to make it heartier, more resistant to bugs, and able to feed more people in developing countries but in the process have turned wheat into something our bodies can barely recognize or process well. For visual proof of the changes, if you look at the wheat of today, it is a full two feet shorter than the wheat of yesteryear.

2. Wheat (like all starchy carbs) spikes your blood sugar levels. It is said that a slice of whole wheat bread has the same reaction in your body as a candy bar. For folks trying to lower their sugar amounts, this is really bad news. Eating bread or pasta spikes your levels and then causes crashes in blood sugar that only can be satisfied by eating more starchy, sugary carbohydrates—creating an addictive, vicious cycle that can doom most any change in eating habits.

3. The protein gluten contained in all wheat can be inflammatory to a large percentage of the population. Many people have an underlying, undiagnosed allergic-type reaction or sensitivity to the protein gluten in wheat, which can cause a host of inflammatory medical problems, including joint pain (arthritis), digestive issues, skin problems, asthma, hay fever, and on and on. The reason gluten-free diets are all the rage now is because when doctors advised clients to go off gluten to test for this allergy/sensitivity, the doctors were stunned to learn that in addition to helping solve the various health issues, their patients lost tons of weight!

4. Wheat is highly addicting and amplifies cravings. Just like its evil twin, processed junk food, many wheat-based products are now engineered in laboratories to appeal to all the pleasure centers of your brain and can create all the effects of an opiate-like addiction. When I first learned of this—I knew immediately they were describing me. Sometimes I would be drawn to the kitchen like a force field in Star Trek and my cravings were so strong, only a piece of toast would quench it. I dreamed of fresh sourdough bread at night. No one had to diagnosis me as a wheat addict!

It is for this last reason that I think wheat is problematic for EVERYBODY, even if you don't think you have a gluten sensitivity. If you eat a candy bar, it is bad for you and spikes your blood sugar and insulin levels. But if you eat a wheat flour cookie (or a sandwich, or a plate of pasta), it will set off a cascade of cravings exponentially worse than the simple carb or sugar number on the label. I guarantee it already has—and in the future definitely will—sabotage any diet you've ever been on or will ever go on again.

For a longest time I fell for the "whole grain wheat products are better for you than refined white wheat flour products" thing. Well, yes, they are minimally better for you than white wheat flour (i.e., they contain more fiber)—BUT that still doesn't make them good for you. Eating "whole grain wheat" does not eliminate ANY of the reasons listed here that wheat is bad for you. This is true no matter how much money is spent on deceptive advertising.

There are many reading materials on this subject on the Internet, pro and con, ever since Melissa Diane Smith published her groundbreaking book *Going Against the Grain* a few years ago, followed by Dr. William Davis's bestselling blockbuster *Wheat*

Belly and now Dr. David Perlmutter's startling *Grain Brain*. At a minimum please check out Dr. Mark Hyman's article available on the internet for the *Huffington Post*, "Three Hidden Ways Wheat Makes You Fat," September 2, 2012. It is short, easy to read, and directly to the point. All these doctors and expert nutritionists also talk about why all the **"gluten-free" junk carbohydrate products on the market can be a disaster for you as well.**

If after doing your own research you are still on the fence—here's what I suggest. Go off wheat for at least two to three months and see what happens. There are no critical nutritional requirements that wheat, whole grain wheat, and all its flour progeny fulfill. It is not "loaded" with protein. Yes, whole grain wheat can supply some fiber to your diet, but nothing that can't be made up in a vastly more nutritious way with the increased level of vegetable and salad eating that will now be part of your plan.

A Word About Wheat Withdrawal: The best way to stop eating wheat is to stop eating wheat completely. Unfortunately this is the one food group that getting rid of it gradually doesn't really work and only prolongs the agony. The withdrawal period can feel anything from uncomfortable to agonizing. I instinctively knew I was a wheat addict, but still the withdrawal symptoms of irritability, overwhelming cravings, and inability to focus took me by surprise. It wasn't until I started crying after a not particularly sad movie when out to dinner with girlfriends that I knew I had gone over the edge. Fortunately my withdrawal only lasted about a week. When you are trying to get off wheat, make sure that that is your **Number One Priority**—not weight loss, not other food rules, and definitely not counting calories.

The more the thought of going off wheat scares you silly, the more you are proving the point about being addicted. As with ending any serious addiction, be prepared—you can use the suggestions under **"Break Glass in Case of Emergency"** (p 46). I almost cracked a couple of times and had some white knuckle experiences. But I had wheat-free crackers, popcorn, and even some slices of wheat-free bread as backstops. I knew I wanted to lessen or eliminate my intake of all those things, and eventually I did, but first things first.

There is Life After Wheat

Once you get off wheat, the lessening of cravings will make eliminating other unhealthy foods seem like child's play in comparison. It truly is the "brass ring" of weight control. The feeling of freedom was exhilarating. **For the first time in my life I felt like I was the one REALLY in control of what I chose to eat.** I would now not trade that feeling for anything in the world.

I know that it can seem almost un-American to not eat wheat, so also get prepared for howls of disbelief and protest from family and friends. But just wait until you go through your transformation...You Will Be Amazed!!!

Processed Food

The easy definition of processed food is "anything made by a corporation and not in your kitchen." It's a very easy concept to understand—not so easy to implement. For example, I am a big fan of pesto sauce that comes in a jar, which technically is a processed food. Only fairly dedicated foodies with time on their hands can keep all the ingredients for fresh pesto and whip them up quickly every time this very valuable, favorable group of ingredients can help flavor a dish or soup you are cooking. So clearly, exceptions are in order—but please read the labels of any such sauces or other short-cuts to keep the added chemicals, sugars, and additives to a minimum.

There is a new threat from the Big Food Corporations looming on the horizon, but first a little history. About twenty years ago, fats (especially saturated fats) were thought to be THE diet villains. So the food industry responded by creating and marketing their made-in-the-lab food as "low fat." Instead of the fats, they loaded their products up with lots of addictive carbohydrates and sugars, which has led directly to the obesity epidemic we are now facing.

It is happening again. Similarly now that "gluten free" is all the rage, they are replacing wheat flour–based processed food with all sorts of other junk made-in-the-lab carbohydrates and...wait for it...still a lot of sugar! I've had women tell me "I tried gluten free but it didn't work for me." when all they did was replace a package of processed wheat flour cookies with other processed flour cookies made from lots of refined sugars and goodness knows what else. Sadly, it doesn't work that way. If you cook or bake with flour, use instead only quality, minimally processed, low-carb single ingredient flours like ground flax, coconut and almond flour.

In a pinch, the one exception to premade food I like is the **Amy's** line of frozen foods. Made by a company in California with family-owned superior standards, they are vegetarian, as much as possible organic, and don't rely on unhealthy additives. For those of you who might be skeptical ANY frozen entre can be healthy – I invite you to compare the ingredient portion of the label of an

Amy's meal with a similar entre of one the other allegedly healthy or "lite" frozen meals. Their Mexican and Indian meals are excellent and they are becoming more readily available in most quality grocery stores. Of course, because you are going off wheat, choose only the wheat/gluten-free varieties. And don't overdo it!

However, if America's largest corporations don't cook your food—YOU will have to! Don't worry. That's where I come in to help you learn the ropes. (See Chapter 13, "**Keeping the Cooking Simple**.")

Sugar

By now it's common knowledge that all forms of white or brown sugar are bad for you. Artificial sweeteners are even worse, and even so-called "natural" or low-calorie sweeteners processed in a lab (yes...that includes agave and stevia) are bad for you. They are all bad for you. So the question becomes...Which is the least bad for you? I believe it is **raw, unprocessed organic bees' honey**, which is creamy and dense as opposed to clear and golden colored. It is not processed in a lab. It is in a similar state to the sweetener that was stolen from bee hives by our cavemen ancestors a long, long time ago, so it is not unknown to the human digestive system. And as a bit of a bonus, it contains antioxidants.

So if sugar is so bad for you, why would I say even a small amount is excusable? Because I personally believe it is not possible for many people to stick to an eating plan that does not allow for a little added sweetness other than fruit, at least in the beginning. I think it is fine for TV doctors and other experts with the apparent willpower of Spartan soldiers to say, "No, nope, not ever—not one little drop of sugar," but I think that is an extremely high standard for most of us mere mortals to live up to. If the standard is too awfully difficult to achieve—then it is tailor-made for cheating and falling off the wagon. And lord knows, falling off the wagon Big Time with cookies, cake, and dairy fat ice creams (which are all so wrong on so many different levels) could lead to much bigger problems for what you really want—a long-term lifestyle change.

If you can get off sugar completely, WONDERFUL!!!! DO IT!!!! But I also have room for an approach that allows for human frailties and for slower reduction of sugar. If you are anything like me, my sugar taste buds were so out of whack from years of soda and artificial sweeteners that I couldn't appreciate the natural sweet goodness of fruits. I thought eating an apple was like eating cardboard. Now I relish apples and other fruits because I have realigned my taste buds. So I say, use a little honey in your coffee, tea, or dessert if you want and reduce it as much as possible as soon as you can.

6
Cravings versus Calories

I don't know how many times I had to learn this lesson, but I finally did. **Eating to become healthy is different than eating to lose weight.** If you eat to be healthy, you will almost invariably lose weight. But if you eat only to lose weight, it will almost always be unhealthy for you, whether you lose weight or not.

A debate has erupted in the diet/nutrition community now that healthy eating has also become a diet craze. It used to be accepted gospel that dieting was a function of "calories in—calories out." In other words, if you expended more calories a day (presumably by upping your exercise level) than you took in (by eating less food), you would lose weight. The quality of the food was rarely questioned. Based on this theory, a generation of women started trying to exercise more and eating largely prepackaged, low-fat processed foods no matter what was in them as long as the total calorie count for the day was around 1,000 calories. And usually they lost the battle.

Thankfully, this whole theory is now in rapid decline for several very good reasons:

1. **It is not the QUANTITY of calories you consume that make a difference—it is the QUALITY of the calories.** In the frozen food section of your supermarket there are all sorts of meal and dessert substitutes that were originally designed for our convenience. Now they are making us sick and obese in large numbers. The "low-calorie" selections advertised as "light" and "lean" are diet and nutrition disasters. For a while, I fell victim to their siren song of low-calorie ease. You could just pop them in the microwave and eat three of them a day for less than 1,000 calories. But you would be eating lots of extremely un-nutritious junk masquerading as food, such as excess salt, preservatives, gluten, nitrates, other unnecessary chemicals, sugars...well you get the point. Just read the ingredient labels. And even worse, they are now designed to addict you and keep you coming back for more junk.

2. If your body doesn't get the nutrition it needs from real food—fruits and vegetables and quality fats and proteins—it will literally fight back against you in a multitude of ways, including listlessness, hunger, and cravings. If kept up long enough, it will cause disease and sickness. At the risk of overstating the obvious – why would you want to purposefully harm your body?

3. Along these same lines...Does anybody think a wheat flour, dairy milk, and sugar pancake (290 calories) is as good for you as an egg, veggie, and avocado omelet (290 calories)?! One of these your body will rejoice in and will keep you filled up for hours—the other it will consider crummy, sugary goo and will punish you for eating it by sending it straight to your belly in the form of ugly yellow belly fat. **And** it will make you hungry again in an hour or

34

two. Heck, sprinkle some cheese in the omelet and it's still infinitely healthier than the pancake would be for just a few more calories!

Any weight you lose from a low-calorie diet will be gained back eventually as your body struggles to regain its former status where it may have been unhealthy, but at least it wasn't hungry.

So I say—be mindful and aware of calories and try to save them where you can. But do not be overly obsessed with counting them or, for that matter, "points." Use that time instead to get in the kitchen and make yourself some quick, easy, and filling **real** food.

7
Making Good Choices Is the Key

~~~~~~

This book is not meant to be a self-help book on the very real issues of emotional overeating and food addiction. There are dozens of excellent books on this subject, and I invite you to investigate them. This cookbook contains my suggestions for how to get healthier (and probably lose weight) by eating healthier and by making it easier to do so. Nothing more, nothing less.

I guess because I am not a TV expert or doctor, I would not expect absolute perfection from anyone reading this book. That is why I have **"The 90/10 Rule"** and the **"Break Glass in Case of Emergency"** (p. 46) suggestions.

I and the experts can give you information and tools, but no one can make the choices for you.

One thing throughout this journey I have learned to be absolutely true: The mental muscle for making good choices about food is one that needs to be exercised to get strong. If, for the longest time, you have walked in the kitchen and mindlessly grabbed anything that appealed to you—mostly junk foods—you are going to need practice making good choices.

Every time you walk into the kitchen, every time you look at a restaurant menu—you will have a series of important decisions to make. You need to stop, take a deep breath, and be VERY present when you make those choices. Mindless, thoughtless choices are the worst. Instead, visualize how miserable you were/are versus the strong, healthy person you are/want to be. Hopefully, the vast majority of the time this will lead you to make a good choice for good health. But, if on occasion, you make a bad choice, it does not mean you are a bad person with no willpower or that you have thrown your plan completely out the window. It only means you need to try and make a better choice the next time, one choice at a time. It really is as simple as that and it will get easier and easier.

To the food police, it may sound like I am giving folks excuses to "cheat." I absolutely hate that idea. **There are no cheaters, just as there are no legitimate excuses—only occasional bad choices based on a perceived reality at that time.** I am only acknowledging that folks are human. Mistakes will be made. Don't go all drama queen about it. Just move on and, in the end—persevere!

It can be very helpful to have a buddy or two along with you for the journey so you can seek reinforcement, share notes and research, and in general just have someone to talk to about what you are going through. The concept of shared experiences and emotional support to deal with addictions was started by Alcoholics Anonymous, used with great success by Weight

Watchers, and now championed by the religious-based Daniel Plan. To me, it's not about allegiance to anyone particular food or diet plan, but rather an acknowledgement of the success of shared support among persons who care about each other and are going through much the same challenges as you.

8
Compromises, Setbacks, and Other Issues

~~~~~~~~~

I know that giving up wheat, sodas, and processed food favorites is a big, difficult chore, no matter what anybody says. The feelings of withdrawal can range from slightly uncomfortable to really tough. You want to work hard to develop the mental muscle that will lead to better choices. But every once in a while, things will go wrong.

Falling Off the Wagon

Yes, you want to be extremely rigorous in your adherence to your eating plan, particularly when it comes to wheat because, as described in Chapter 5 "**The Not So Good For You Foods**," wheat = cravings and cravings = wheat in what amounts to a really vicious feedback loop. But unless you are a complete control freak, you understand that life is not lived in a void and mistakes will happen.

First of all, let me try to distinguish between "splurging" and "falling off the wagon." Splurging occurs when you are in complete control, and you allow yourself the ability to have a treat—a small reward for being so good about sticking to your goals. On the other hand, falling off the wagon represents a loss of control, a surrender, and a return to thoughtless, mindless emotional eating. You don't need me to tell you which is which; it has happened to you hundreds of times whenever you have tried to diet.

I am here to say...that falling off the wagon isn't nearly as scary, defeating, or tragic as we make it out to be. If you set up it up psychologically as a major defeat, then it will be. Try to look at it as a setback rather than as a tragedy of major proportions and an excuse to accuse yourself of not being able to stick with anything. Realize that eating healthy and getting healthy really is a PROCESS and that leaning into it gradually will ultimately get more results than drama and hysterics. If you feel yourself about to lose it, it helps to have some less than horrible options thought out ahead. (See **"Break Glass in Case of Emergency"** section later in this Chapter.) Then get right back on the wagon.

Compromises and the 90/10 Rule

As you will quickly notice, within my recipes—I make **small** "compromises" on some of the so-called rules of healthy eating. Examples would be the small amounts of cornstarch or flour contained in the store-bought gravy packets and the sugar in the low-fat whipped cream I use on my **Chocolate Frozen Banana Treat**. This could cause unhappy comments from the food police critics and bloggers alike. Tough. I make no apologies and in fact say, **"If you are good 90% of the time, it's better than being bad 100% of the time."** My own personal experience is that, now that I am a safe distance away from my former wheat addiction, eating a bread roll on occasion when out to dinner with friends does not send me into a period of lunacy where I start stuffing my face with all things wheat. My usual splurge item when out to dinner is a baked or mashed potato. I will try not to eat meat if I don't know how the animal was raised, and I will never do a big pasta dish—but going out to dinner is a perfect time to indulge in a lovely seafood item and a baked potato. YUM!

Yes, I too cleaned out my kitchen of most of the offending packaged, processed food items. It was definitely cathartic and symbolized a moving on to the new me. But as an acknowledgment of the old me, I still keep a bag of potato chips on one of my upper shelves. In a very weird way, giving myself permission to eat them if I have to has given me the strength not to. Much like an alcoholic who keeps a bottle of whiskey on the mantle, my bag of potato chips was still there well after a year. You are going to have to trust me on this—the cravings for junky food will disappear quicker than you think, and you will become more and more confident of your ability to make the right choices.

About The Husband and Kids

When it comes to healthy eating, being a single woman, I have the luxury of cooking what I want—and eating when I want. I know that those of you with husbands and families can't always do that. No eating plan is worth strained relations with loved ones—so I say, get prepared to prepare their meal and you eat yours. Yes, I know, all the books say to talk to them and try to bring them on board. Or try to force them to eat what you're eating. But seriously, it is one thing to say no more greasy potato chips—and quite another to say, "No more deli-meat sandwiches or cookies from a package." They will look at you like you are crazy and just stepped off the Mother Ship. I have a wonderful friend who still cooks her husband his favorite meatloaf and then goes about preparing her own dinner. Only now she uses grass-fed beef and wheat-free bread crumbs, so there are ways to stick stuff in there that they won't notice. Another family favorite could be the **Mistaken Identity Mashed Potatoes.** You will be amazed at how much better fruit looks when it has some **Dreamy Dark Chocolate Sauce** sparingly drizzled over it.

But no need go to war. When they see the changes in you over time—hopefully they will start coming along. I have lucky girlfriends who, when they discussed "going healthy" with their husbands or significant others, were actually surprised by their enthusiasm for trying a different way of eating. Men know they are getting fat and sick too.

If your male partner is still reluctant to join you – try steering him to one of my favorite blogs/websites www.marksdailyapple.com. Mark Sisson is a leading champion of the currently popular Paleo/ Primal food movement. Paleo is stricter and more meat oriented than I choose to be, but I enjoy his blog for interesting, thoughtful, well-researched and provocative articles on a range of cutting edge health subjects. I think he gets it dead right when it comes to issues of building muscle mass, strength training and all that stuff so important to men. Mark REALLY dislikes all grains (ie. wheat) and says "Real Men Eat Salads." Wow!

Added Cost

Get ready for your food budget to take something of a hit when you start to eat healthy. Most items in all my recipes can be purchased at a quality (Publix, Super Ingles, newer Safeway) grocery store—but you will need to buy some items on occasion at a local health food store, Whole Foods, Sprouts, or Trader Joe's, if you are lucky enough to have one nearby. You can justify this small added expense many ways:

First: I don't often get a chance to quote Hippocrates, so here it is! "Let food be thy medicine and medicine be thy food." I will take this concept one step further. Because my overall health has gotten so much better, I save lots of money on prescription co-pays and over-the-counter medications. I no longer need gel pads, special cushions, and all sorts of other products. I have saved a ton by getting healthier.

When a potential customer of a small organic farm complained about the higher cost of organic produce, the farmers' response was "Have you priced cancer lately?" I love that answer.

Second: Think of it this way. Imagine someone said to you "I will sell you the loss of that thirty to seventy-five pounds you've always wanted gone AND I'll make you healthier and feel better as a bonus—but it will cost you $1,000." Who among us wouldn't beg for, borrow, or steal the money to pay for that?! Following a healthier eating style is exactly that same bargain except you get to make little payments over time instead of having to pay in one lump sum...a fantastic deal, I think.

Now here's one thing I can't help you with—the cost of the new clothes you will need when you drop dress sizes! Sorry for that...

Scale Watching

Please, Please, Please, **do not watch the scale.** Your weight will fluctuate wildly over the first few weeks as your body adjusts to new foods. The weight loss for me was the last thing that happened in my journey. As my wise friend Barbara says, "If you set yourself up for failure—then it will happen." Constantly stepping on the scale is the first clue to an unhealthy obsession with weight alone, instead of your health, as a measure of success. You are constantly setting yourself up for failure because science tells us that weight fluctuations can be due to a zillion different factors. If the scale disappoints—you will be disappointed and you might just go off and eat something "comforting" (bad for you) as an act of self-loathing punishment. Is that self-defeating or what?

Your first sign you are losing weight is that your clothes will be fitting better and getting too big for you. Wait for it.

I now weigh myself about once a month at the gym, more for curiosity than anything else. And of course I get weighed at my doctor's office. I used to dread going to the doctor because I would always get a constructive lecture about "how my numbers could improve." That's doctor code for "you really need to lose some weight." Now she is so pleased with my results, I love visiting my doctor!

Traveling

What to do when traveling is the worst nightmare for people like us who have become choosy about what they eat. Gosh, I hate to say it, but I think salads with strong herbal fruit teas are the way to go whenever possible. My good friend Coleen, who travels a lot on business, eats salads without dressing. I, who have much less self-discipline, will indulge in some ranch dressing with a bunch of lemons squeezed in. I will also order a shrimp salad as a way of indulging. Almost every restaurant will have a nice fish item with rice or potato on the menu.

The key to eating when traveling is to try not to get too hungry because that's when stress and limited choices will do you in. I always bring along a "travel kit" with a bunch of pomegranate tea bags, a small jar of my raw honey, and bags of wheat-free crackers (garlic and cinnamon) with some herb goat cheese everywhere I go so I will have something to go with the salads and as emergency snacks. I know it's somewhat boring, but fruit in the form of apples and bananas are available almost everywhere; have them first thing in the morning so you don't get desperate around midmorning.

If you have access to any sort of mini-kitchen and a grocery store, try and travel with a small portable blender and make some smoothies. Don't forget your straws! Most hotels have a microwave somewhere for soups and your homemade leftover meals. My little packets of bouillon by Savory Choice have been lifesavers on more than one occasion. Other than that—do the best you can and realize life is about living it to the fullest. This is my consolation mantra after my whole plan goes out the window on occasion, which happens generally on Thanksgiving and Christmas.

Friends

If I were you, I would avoid making an announcement to all your friends that you are starting a new, healthy eating style. Why bother? You are not doing this for attention or accolades. Just do it. Hardly anyone will notice the slightly different choices you are making at a restaurant. Likewise, please, please, do not turn into one of "those people" who gets all preachy and turns up their nose at what their friends and family are eating. You will be considered obnoxious, and rightly so. Once again, let the results speak for themselves, and gently answer questions when asked. Just keep on your own path and maybe, just maybe, be an example for others who might be needier for your suggestions than you suspect. I went from answering questions when asked to giving cooking classes to curious friends at my home. It is so much more gratifying to assist friends in their journey than it is to turn into one of the dreaded food police and drive folks away.

Break Glass in Case of Emergency

When you feel a diet-busting binge coming on—bad day at work, your hormones are out of whack, your boyfriend's a jerk—better to be prepared than fall off the wagon entirely. Here are some suggestions of what to do to get through it. Then the next day, pick yourself up, dust yourself off, and get back in the game with a morning **Basic Berry Smoothie** (p. 80) **and a cup of Savory Vegetable Soup (**p. 94**).**

Wolfgang Puck's free-range chicken and wild rice organic soup: Always have a can available. Poach an egg in it if it needs a little something extra.

Cheesy Brussels sprouts: Make a large bowl of your favorite vegetable (for me it's Brussels sprouts) and then add one-third to one-half of a package of Amy's gluten-free macaroni and cheese... it's fewer than 200 calories and totally fills you up. If the macaroni and cheese is too goopy for you, transfer to some nonstick tin foil and broil for about eight minutes until the top starts turning brown and crispy. Yum! (see p.108 for more detailed recipe)

Fruit: dipped in **Dreamy Dark Chocolate Sauce** with a little whipped cream.

Sami's Bakery millet sourdough bread: Of course, you want to eventually eliminate bread and most flours altogether, but there are just some times when nothing else other than a piece of toasted bread will do. This brand of bread actually tastes like bread but is not made from wheat. Order online at www.samis-bakery.com and keep in the freezer for emergencies.

Fried egg sandwich: Scramble or fry a broken egg with a little spray olive oil and fry flat. Toast one piece of millet or other wheat-free bread with a little butter and eat open-faced. This sandwich satisfies very primal urges without totally falling off the wagon.

Popcorn: When all else fails, and volume matters, go ahead and have a bowl. They now make non-GMO organic popcorn! It won't kill you, and you can eat virtually all you want without the guilt that you binged on one of the Not So Good For You foods. Drizzle with a little real butter if need be.

Pasta: If you absolutely must have some pasta, try the brands that are made entirely of beans instead of substitute starchy grain flours. There is a brand of black and red bean pasta named Tolerant sold in health food stores and by Amazon.com that is actually quite good. You may need to experiment with the cooking times to get the texture just right.

Ice cream: Try mashed frozen bananas with walnuts and **Dreamy Dark Chocolate Sauce** (p.132). If this doesn't work, try the Amy's or SO brand coconut vanilla ice cream and put over some warmed up frozen peaches, cinnamon and walnuts for a peach cobbler treat. The chocolate variety actually tastes very creamy and chocolaty (Is that a word?!?! If not, it should be.).

Go take a walk. WHEW!

9
Pump up the Volume

~~~~~

Women have been trying to lose weight for decades...My mom and her crowd had their fad diets of the day. She particularly liked "The Drinking Man's Diet" for reasons that could be the subject of a whole other book. But one diet that has been around in one form or another for a long time with good reason is Volumetrics. This is a weird name for a diet concept that keeps getting reprised in one fashion or another decade after decade because it is so darn effective!

Simply put, Volumetrics stresses stuffing low-calorie ingredients in everything you make so you can eat more and alleviate hunger. We all know hunger and cravings are our biggest enemies when trying to change eating habits. Throw "portion control" out the window forever by using this tried-and-true method of alleviating hunger. The most obvious examples of this concept are putting chopped-up cooked veggies in your soups and meals and lots of mushrooms and sprouts in your salad. But let me give you some other, more modern-day examples:

Smoothies: Sticking as much raw, adult or baby spinach as you can in your **Basic Berry Smoothie** (p. 80) is brilliant! Spinach has tons of good nutrition (calcium, fiber), and somehow the flavor doesn't show up when matched against fruit. Popeye would be proud of you!

Diana's Deviled Egg Spread: Yes, of course, you must use a little mayo to put in with the egg yolks. But why not throw in some hard-boiled egg whites, celery, and sliced green onion? You can literally double the volume for almost no calories, lower the cholesterol significantly—and add crunch and flavor.

Soups: OK, here comes my favorite. When you make soups or sauces, put TONS of onions and garlic in them. Onions and garlic are loaded with good nutrients and antioxidants. But also as important, I think, is the added flavor they give everything without the need for as much added salt. If you are overweight, you probably have been having blood pressure "issues," and the less salt the better. Once this Dynamic Duo has added a lot of flavor to your soup stock, you can then turn that easily into a lower-salt sauce/gravy for pouring over your veggies and rice.

The point is—Get Creative! Never run out of raw spinach, green and other types of onions, celery, hard-boiled egg whites, and garlic, and put these in absolutely everything. Think Outside the Box—canned water chestnuts add wonderful, mysterious crunch to all sorts of dishes. Hearts of palm make a fantastic tasty addition to any salad. Let your imagination run wild...

10
Why I Am a Flexitarian

~~~~~~~

Meat (defined here as beef, pork, and poultry) can be a main source of **protein**, an essential nutritional component that our bodies need for all sorts of things including energy and healthy cell growth. It also contains some amino acids that can be difficult to get from any other food source. It has no sugar or carbs. By and large we enjoy meat, it helps to fill us up, and most of us have eaten it our whole lives.

HOWEVER, meats as commonly produced in large factory farms have some very real health downsides. They are high in omega-6 fatty acids, which promote inflammation. Fish and seafood, on the other hand, contain omega-3 fatty acids, which contribute to a lessening of inflammation. That is why fish and krill oil capsules are routinely recommended for heart and joint health and pain relief.

The large quantities of meat that are consumed in the Standard American Diet (SAD) are way too much, out of balance, and unhealthy. As Americans we consume, on average, at least a twenty-to-one ratio of omega-6 to omega-3, whereas a four-to-one (land based) or one-to-four (sea/ocean based) ratio is the norm in much healthier, non-industrialized populations. Out-of-balance omega-6 fatty acids in your own diet can lead to arthritis, heart disease, diabetes, and a whole host of other medical problems that stem from low-level but chronic, systemic inflammation.

One of reasons factory-farmed animals have such a high level of omega-6 fatty acids is that they are fed a diet of higher fat content, pesticide-sprayed, cheap corn and soy products. This is done to fatten them up (more $ in profits for heavier animals)—and then you wind up being the one who is "fattened up." For much the same reason, dairy cows are given growth hormones so they will produce more milk. These hormones have been outlawed in Europe and Canada and have been linked to gynecological cancers.

Another problem is that factory-farmed animals are routinely given antibiotics. Poultry and pork in particular are housed in such small cages and raised so close together that it promotes disease sharing in their populations. So the industry gives them antibiotics to prevent disease—it doesn't matter if they are actually sick or not. This routine overuse of antibiotics has been a large contributor to the development of antibiotic-resistant "superbugs," which are killing people right now in and out of the hospital.

And these are just the highlights of some of the more commonly accepted problems. For years I turned a blind eye to these issues because I enjoyed cooking with and eating meat, and I saw no other alternative other than vegetarianism. I have many friends who are vegans and vegetarians, and I admire that lifestyle. I admired it and aspired to it so much that I would try it out myself from time to time, but each time I would slip back to eating meat.

Thankfully, a third choice is now emerging called Flexitarianism. As generally accepted, this somewhat awkward label applies to people who eat less meat in their meals and eat meat only from more humanely raised **and therefore more healthy** animals. That is now me. Humanely raised meat is labeled as free-range chicken, grass-fed beef, or pasture-raised pork. The animals are allowed to eat food that is more natural to them (i.e., grass-fed beef cows get to eat grass and hay, which lessens the amount of omega-6 fats present in their grain- and soy-fed cousins). It also involves choosing organic dairy products produced by cows who are not given added hormones to stimulate their milk production. As well, be on the lookout for meat and dairy products labeled antibiotic free.

How do you locate this healthier meat? Whole Foods grocery stores use an internationally recognized numerical rating of how their fresh meat is raised, using numbers 1 through 5 on a scale, with 5+ being the most humanely raised meat. www.wholefoodsmarket.com (Animal Welfare Standards). I now purchase only meat that is raised the equivalent to a 4 or a 5 on this scale. If I have to drive an hour once a month to a Whole Foods, buy it fresh, put it in a cooler, transport it home, and freeze it for use throughout the month—I will do it. Trader Joe's also offers some good choices. Many of you are lucky enough to a real farmer's market as an available option. For those of you who would argue that this certainly is not quick and easy shopping, I am happy to report that as demand is increasing, quality grocery stores are now at least offering grass-fed ground beef and free-range chicken meat and eggs. A friend of mine even reported buying cage-free, antibiotic-free chicken breasts at Walmart! I invite you to explore these options.

Yes, absolutely these products are a little more expensive. But please keep in mind the "Food as Medicine" argument. Also, if you are eating healthy, the meat portion of your meal should now be a side dish as opposed to the main course. Therefore the total meat part of your food bill should not increase at all. The healthiest of all the world's populations (Asia before the Colonel Sanders and McNugget Invasion, the Mediterranean, etc.) eat this way and have much lower rates of heart disease, cancer, and diabetes.

Before all my vegetarian friends take me off their Christmas card list for giving folks a pass to eat meat, I would argue that there are folks who, like me, would be eating meat anyway—we just should choose better. I realize the verification and certification process for grass-fed and free-range/roaming producers is not perfect. It is truly an evolving movement. I may be hopelessly naïve, but I believe that farmers and ranchers who attempt and get these certifications have made a lifestyle choice to treat their animals better and therefore make their meat healthier. And just as with organic farmers, I think those of us who are consumers should reward them for their efforts to help make us healthier. One of the only ways for us regular folks to "vote" on this issue is with our pocketbooks. Making the best choice about the animal products you cook with will improve the lives of the animals, your food experience, and your health!

Additional Sources of Protein

Hemp protein powder: This is a green vegetable powder that is virtually tasteless. I put a tablespoon in almost everything I make, especially my soups and smoothies. The very popular whey protein powder comes from dairy cow cheese by-products so if you are avoiding dairy, you want to be aware of that.

Egg whites: See **Diana's Deviled Egg Spread** (p. 101)

Nuts and seeds: See **Super Seeds** (p. 85)

Edamame: See **Tasty Mixed Vegetables** (p. 82)

Beans: See **Three-Bean Lentil Soup** (p. 99)

11
It's Really Not That Complicated...

...it really isn't. Here are the central goals:

1. **Avoid wheat in all its forms, including "whole grain."**

2. **Eat as much stuff from green vegetables and berries/fruit as you can possibly manage.** Make everything else lesser parts of your diet.

3. **Cook your own food.** That way you control your fat, salt, and sugar content, which all should be kept to a minimum.

4. **Limit your toxic exposure.** Eat organic when possible. Choose humanely raised meat. Never microwave plastic. Drink purified water and lots of it.

5. **Quit obsessing over food.** Make simple, easy choices so you can get on with the other wonderful things in your life.

Many of the diet/healthy eating plans you may have looked at have charts, schedules, graphs, point counting, journal keeping, eating certain foods at different times of the day, eating different foods on different days of the week, and on and on and on. That may be fine for folks who need a certain amount of structure to reinforce discipline. All of that did not appeal to me, as is obvious by my approach in this book. One of my goals was to get unobsessed about food and eating—and keeping these five simple rules in the front of my mind when faced with food choices really helped.

12
Exercise

This is going to be the shortest chapter in this book because there are so many other really good other books and DVDs on this subject.

If you have an exercise plan you like—stick with it. I lost weight and got healthy without substantially increasing the amount of my exercise. I believe in exercise to increase one's overall wellness and health, but I do not believe you have to hit the gym for 40 minutes of kill-yourself aerobic workouts to lose weight.

But if you do not exercise at all, try these things:

Walk as fast as is comfortable for you twenty to thirty minutes a day four to five times a week. Take some music with you!

Afterward, lay on the ground and roll and stretch and flex every joint in your body. Do easy leg lifts, paying special attention to strengthening the core muscles in your abdomen. Stretch your arms and shoulders as high as you can. Just rejoice in feeling every part of your body loosen up and not be so stiff.

Take up an outdoor hobby you like—for example, swimming, golf, being with animals, gardening, and so on.

JUST MOVE MORE!

13
Keeping the
Cooking Simple

It's amazing that one single activity, cooking, evokes such rapture in some people and absolute loathing in others. On a scale, I am a little closer to the rapture side—I am a person who now views cooking as a relaxing, creative outlet that feeds both my body and my soul. Because I have come to see how directly it has led to my lessening of pain <u>and</u> weight, and how it has improved the quality of my life so significantly, I actually now look forward to spending time in the kitchen.

But I am well aware there are many folks on the other side of the scale. They view cooking in the same way as doing the laundry and making up the bed...at some point necessary, but to be avoided whenever possible.

Then there are the folks who have always been intimidated by cooking, either because they did not grow up in families where cooking was a part of their tradition or because they have just been too busy with other priorities to take an interest in it. So they are unsure of themselves in the kitchen but instinctively know they are going to have to up their game if they want to eat healthier.

This book is written primarily for these folks. Real health food "foodies" have dozens of books from which to choose with far more complicated, time-consuming, and dazzling recipes in them, and I love looking through them from time to time. But when you are just starting out, quick and easy is the way to go. I unapologetically go overboard to explain the how-to part of my recipes in great detail. If you ever have any questions about anything that comes up when trying my recipes, please don't hesitate to e-mail me at:

nopasta@outlook.com

The unvarnished truth remains that if you are going to give up most processed food, which is concocted by corporations in a laboratory and factory setting for your convenience, you are just going to have to spend more time in your own kitchen making **real** food. After a bit of a learning curve, you can reduce this time to about five or six hours a week. Here's how:

- Try and dedicate a three- to four-hour block of time once a week to get the bulk of your cooking done. That way you can accomplish several tasks at one time, and preparing meals throughout the rest of the week becomes a breeze. I would suggest breaking up major grocery shopping trips and cooking into two separate projects only because doing the two on the same evening or day can be tiring.

- Make most of your vegetables (**Tasty Mixed Vegetables** p. 82) ahead for five days.

- Make your rice ahead for a few days. It's very easy to cook rice (**Perfect Rice Every Time** p. 86).

- Cook your soup stocks and broths when you cook your vegetables, use them over and over again every time you cook more vegetables, and refrigerate them in glass jars for soups and snacks to heat up quickly.

- Every time you cook a seafood or meat portion (generally with sauce or gravy) for your meals, make enough for three or four meals to use as leftovers.

- In order to make a portion of meat go further, taste better and cook quicker, try an Asian cooking trick used in stir fry. Before sautéing (frying), slice your raw meat (chicken, pork or beef) with a very sharp knife on a diagonal angle, in very thin slices. Place in a hot pan with just a little coconut or olive oil, sauté and flip each slice once and they're done in a just a minute or two.

- If the thought of making smoothies every morning is too complicated, then try this. Smoothies can last for two, even three days in tightly lidded containers. Every other night make enough smoothie for two mornings and refrigerate. Pull it out in the morning, stick a straw in it and heat up some Savory Vegetable Soup up in the microwave. Breakfast can take less than five minutes.

- With all due respect to Rachel Ray, I generally use minced garlic from a jar. I use a ton of garlic and don't have the time or the patience to peel, chop, or grate as much of this amazing plant/herb as I use it in most every recipe. I want to be able to put spoonfuls in my stocks, broths, and soups without getting my fingers all smelly.

- All (and I do mean ALL) measurements in my recipes are approximate and are all "to taste." Please feel absolute flexibility to experiment with differing amounts of flavoring and ingredients to make the recipes work for you and be tasty for YOU. After all – you are the one who is going to have to eat them! Don't forget—recipes are really just a concept or idea—they need your flair to come to life.

If you really are all thumbs in the kitchen, can I suggest a wonderful investment for you? Mark Bittman's book *How to Cook Everything— The Basics—With 1,000 Photos* unravels all the mysteries of the kitchen—with pictures!

14
Breakfast: The Most Important (and Problematic) Meal of the Day

~~~~~~

Breakfast was always an issue for me. I never wanted to eat it because I wasn't generally hungry first thing in the morning, and the thought of the standard American breakfast made me slightly nauseous. There are basically two choices. One is an egg together with a greasy, processed, nitrated, salted piece of meat (bacon or sausage) and some sort of fried-in-grease potato thingie or toast (fats, starch or wheat) **OR** choice two is a bowl of cereal with milk. Even if you do granola and skim milk—it's still wheat or grains in a very rough form, sugar, and dairy. I now realize that my body didn't want any of those things, and the slightly nauseous feeling I had was its way of trying to tell me that none of those things were appreciated by it and—in fact—would be rapidly rejected by my body if I tried to force them down.

So inevitably I would skip breakfast and head off to work on an empty stomach. Then I would generally be confronted with the **worst possible alternative**—doughnuts and pastries (sugar, wheat, REALLY bad fats) that some well-intentioned person had brought in for everyone. This practice gets particularly horrendous around the holidays in winter. By midmorning, because by now my body was starving, I would usually succumb—setting off a chain of events for the day: still starving by lunch, so I craved starchy carbs... needing to snack every few hours to keep my energy up...all the time my inflammation and digestive system were raging because my body had been assaulted by stuff it didn't want, certainly didn't need, and, as I have now learned, was literally toxic to it.

So now here's what I have for breakfast almost every day. A **Basic Berry Smoothie** (p. 80) and a mug of **Savory Vegetable Soup** (p. 94). Because there is nothing bad for you in either item, and both are loaded with nutrition and antioxidants, your body is happy and grateful. They are both in liquid form, so it is easy for your digestive system to absorb. And it FILLS YOU UP so you can easily pass on those doughnut-type lumps of fat and other poisonous objects in the office break room. And here's the best part—because your cravings have been greatly diminished from your whole new eating style, you stay filled up until you can have a healthy lunch. I have a cut up apple (mostly skin part where all the nutrition is) sometime midmorning and am good to go until about one in the afternoon—Salad Time!

If you need more substance, poach an egg in your soup and/or add some veggies and brown rice. I put torn up pieces of nori (Japanese seaweed that is used to roll up sushi) for a unique salt-like flavor and micronutrients without much sodium. Get creative! Another possibility is a Cream of Rice–type warm cereal with some coconut milk and mashed fresh or frozen berries. Oats are a variation of wheat and generally have gluten in them, but you can find steel cut oats without gluten. If you really feel you need an egg dish, try an omelet or scramble with any sautéed veggies you choose. For a fancier, brunch-type meal, try **Veggie and Potato Frittata** (p. 112) or **Egg Foo Young** (p. 106).

Please think about being gentle on your digestive system and do your body a favor—don't assault it with junk first thing in the morning. It won't go well the rest of the day!

15
Mix-and-Match
Meal Plans and
the Importance
of Leftovers

~~~~

Here is how easy it can be to eat healthy throughout the day:

Breakfast: See previous chapter.

Lunch: A Salad (see p. 102)

Dinner: Assemble a **Main Dish** meal.

Assembling a Main Dish meal:

15%–25% lean, healthy raised chicken, beef, pork, seafood, or tofu

15%–20% carbohydrate – brown or other rice, beans, quinoa, sweet potato (**Perfect Rice Every Time** or **Mistaken Identity Mashed Potatoes**)

55%–65% vegetables (**Tasty Mixed Vegetables**)

Cover with an inventive, flavorful sauce or gravy (**Basic Sauces and Gravies**) and if you want, sprinkle with **Super Seeds**.

There you have it! Simple as can be and there can be hundreds of variations on this theme limited only by your imagination.

Besides tofu, as another vegetarian option instead of meat or as a timesaver – don't forget the possibility of using a portion of an Amy's frozen food entre such as Cheese or Bean Enchiladas, Gluten-free Lasagna and so forth. For a single serving, I cook the entire package and then use one third in the meal I intend to eat at the time, and refrigerate the rest to heat up another time.

A word about lunch. I know it's hard if you've had a rough or busy morning at work to face eating a salad at lunch. It is nourishing but sometimes not that satisfying. You don't want to fall off the wagon with a wheat bread, salted/nitrated deli meat sandwich or pizza slice or other horrible option lurking around the corner at a fast food joint. So here's how I did it. I always brought with me an already assembled **Main Dish** meal in a microwaveable container to work to be stored in the refrigerator. If a salad for lunch sounded like a good option, I had it. Goody for me! Then I would just take the **Main Dish** meal home with me and have it for dinner. That way you always have options which is so important to sticking to a healthy eating plan.

At this point I would like to give a nod to the idea of **routine** in planning for meals. The more you can take indecisiveness out of the picture, the less opportunity you have for mindless eating. For example, it lowered my morning stress by always having a smoothie and soup as my primary, go-to option in the morning. Always try and have stuff available to make some sort of salad. Try to always have leftover rice and vegetables around. Then all you have to decide on is a meat/seafood side dish and a complimentary easy flavorful sauce/ gravy. I don't mean to imply you should become a robot—but taking a lot of guesswork and decision making out of the whole process will work to your advantage over the long run.

The Importance Of Leftovers

The importance of leftovers cannot be overstressed. Anytime you cook you should consider doubling or tripling the recipe to use later for leftovers. Why? So you don't have to spend as much time in the kitchen and make a whole new meal each time from scratch. Of course, this saves time. But an even more important concept comes into play:

In order to avoid bad choices, you must have readily available good tasting healthy choices already in the kitchen!

If you have leftover healthy meals and snacks already available— which are easy to heat up and satisfying to eat—you can more easily avoid a very bad choice. Planning ahead is always very helpful.

16
What and
Where to Buy

~~~~~~~

Health Food Stores

OK, OK...I know I promised that you would not have to buy a lot of fancy ingredients. And I think I have largely adhered to that promise in the recipes. But there are just a few things that are generally not found in regular grocery stores that you may need to go an Earth Fare, Whole Foods, Sprouts, or neighborhood health food store to buy about once a month. Having said that, a lot of quality grocery stores are now stepping up their game in providing healthy specialty items, and you may be able to find these items on their shelves if you know where to look or ask for them.

Raw organic bees' honey: The less processed, the better. The honey should be dense and cream colored instead of golden and clear.

Organic low-sodium gluten-free tamari sauce: Use instead of the old-fashioned standard soy sauce.

Organic gluten-free vegetarian gravy packets (see p. 86)

Organic, non-GMO popcorn: I would get plain and add your own salt and butter to taste.

Hemp protein powder: This is a green, virtually tasteless boost of protein that I find easy to slip into all my soups and smoothies.

Regular Grocery Store

Dairy milk substitute: Almond or coconut are the best choices. Make sure you get the unsweetened varieties, not those with flavor or sugar added.

Garlic: I buy it in big jars either minced or crushed.

Coconut oil

Olive oil

Vegetable bouillon: I like the Better than Bouillon brand, but Savory Choice packets are good too. Get low sodium where available.

Fruit tea: Purchase flavors of your choice. Berry of some type works best. Avoid caffeine.

Cornstarch: Look for non-GMO.

Brown rice: I like jasmine the best but basmati is good too.

Wild rice

Dark cocoa powder

Cage-free or free range eggs

Seeds and nuts

Coconut flour

Flax Seed Meal: I like Bob's Red Mill golden whole ground variety best.

Produce Section

Vegetables: Any that you like!

Fruit

Apples

Celery

Green onions

Lemons

Berries: Blueberry, blackberry, raspberry – All great in smoothies and desserts.

Bananas

Fresh Salsa: in the produce section.

Pomegranate juice: Make sure the juice you are purchasing contains ALL pomegranates, no apple or grape juice. Also look for no added sugar.

Avocados: You can easily ripen by putting in a brown paper bag for a couple of days.

Seasonings and Things
to Have Around to Use
in Almost Everything

Low-sodium gluten free organic tamari sauce	Lemon
Garlic, minced or crushed	Garlic granules (salt free)
Chicken bouillon (No Chicken vegan A-OK)	Pesto sauce
Vegetable bouillon	
Celery and green onion	Italian seasoning (salt free)
Olive oil	Mexican hot sauce
Coconut oil	Fresh salsa

Frozen Section

Berries and fruit

Shelled non-GMO edamame

Salmon (Pacific wild caught is best) and other seafood

Amy's Gluten Free Entrees

Nonfood Items Handy to Have Around

Blender

Nonstick tin foil: This is an excellent invention!

Mini-chopper/blender (food processor): I don't even own one of those big food processors; they always looked very complicated to me, with a lot of moving parts. If I had more mouths to feed, I would probably get one, but I don't—so the mini version works just fine for me, even if sometimes I have to do two batches. Cuisinart and Oster both make good ones.

Large-mouth funnel: For straining the stocks and broths back into jars after using to cook vegetables or meat. I found a great one in the automotive section of Walmart.

Metal strainers: It is best not to put really hot food through any kind of plastic, including colanders. You will need a metal strainer with fine netting to strain your soups and make the cauliflower substitute recipes, **Mistaken Identity Mashed Potatoes** and **Amazing Pizza Crust**.

Great Online Shopping

www.samisbakery.com: This site has fantastic crackers—wheat-free millet and flax crackers in garlic and cinnamon are my favorites. Their sourdough millet bread is excellent if you must have some bread around. It keeps very well in the freezer for emergencies. Yes, it's expensive—which is a good deterrent from eating too much!

www.soupsonline.com: This site provides bouillons of every possible flavor—try to get low sodium. I like the Better than Bouillon brand for everyday cooking, and their No Chicken Base is a favorite staple.

www.amazon.com: If you can't find something you are looking for anywhere else, try putting it in the search box and you will be amazed what shows up. They are a wonderful resource for things you can't find in any of your grocery stores, such as vegetarian pesto sauce (believe it not, most pesto sauces contain something called rennet, which is an enzyme made from the lining of baby cows' stomachs...YUCK!). I like some more exotic Indian food flavors like tandoori and masala and I can find many different ethnic flavoring sauces at this website.

17
Recipes

~~~~~~~~

Let's Get Cooking!

Pomegranate Tea Drink

Plain, clean water should be your first hydration choice, and you should drink a lot of it. You also need to get rid of the SODAS and sugary fruit juices as one of the first steps to get rid of cravings and stop ingesting harmful processed sugars and artificial sweeteners. You can use this pomegranate tea drink when you feel the need for something slightly sweet that will satisfy in the same way as a soda or juice. It doesn't taste like iced tea; it should instead taste like a glass of slightly weak, fresh fruit juice—but it does not have all the junk sugars (corn syrup or artificial sweeteners) found in everything else I researched or tried to buy.

In a 2 cup Pyrex glass measuring pitcher put:

2 cups fresh cold water

4–5 bags Bigelow Pomegranate Pizzazz fruit tea (for other tea possibilities see suggestions later in this recipe)

Put in microwave for 3 to 4 minutes. It should get to the point of boiling, but not quite boil. Remove from microwave and add:

1–2 tsp. raw, unprocessed organic honey, to taste. Stir honey in tea until thoroughly melted and then let tea and honey steep for about half an hour.

Have two 14 - 16 oz. bottles ready. **Glass** salad dressing bottles are perfect to use over and over again. In each bottle put:

1/4 cup pomegranate juice (Must be 100% pomegranate juice, no apple, grape, or "other juices," and no added sugars of any kind. Made from concentrate is OK. I like the POM brand, which is in the hourglass-shaped bottles and found almost everywhere.)

When tea has cooled, remove and squeeze tea bags into tea. Pour tea into the two glass containers, splitting the tea evenly. You will have two containers filled about two-thirds full. Fill almost to the top with regular water or **carbonated**, no sugar added, flavorless water if you want a fizzy texture. Place cap on tightly and refrigerate.

Tips: Eventually you want to lessen your reliance on sweets, even raw honey. But your taste buds need to go through "detox," and this is a natural way to do it. Over the course of days and weeks, use a bit less of the honey. I could never make it to going entirely without—I got to about 1/2 a teaspoon, and that is where I am today. Also, you can adjust the strength of the fruit taste by adding or removing a tea bag. You can mix and match flavors by adding interesting tea flavors!

When thoroughly chilled you can put it in plastic containers and take with you everywhere in lunch cooler boxes. I whip one out at friends' houses, at parties, when I travel—whenever I might be confronted with a soda option. Served over ice, with a splash of lime—it is perfection. People will want to know what you are drinking—let them taste it first, and they will rarely guess tea. Then tell them—and we will get the Whole World off Sodas!

Tea choices: Can be used in any combination. Most grocery stores carry at least one of these, and all are available online.

Bigelow:	Pomegranate Pizzazz
	Red Raspberry
Twining's:	Red Raspberry & Pomegranate
	Wild Berries
Celestial:	Black Cherry

Juice choices: Needs to be all pure juice with no added sugar. Read ingredient label carefully!

Pomegranate (with blueberry or cherry OK)

Cranberry

Black cherry

Basic Berry Smoothie

The berry or fruit smoothie is a basic building block for a healthy eating lifestyle. Delicious for breakfast with a cup of **Savory Vegetable Soup** (p. 94) or scrambled eggs.

You do not need a fancy, expensive juicer or blender to make a smoothie. A basic, old-fashioned bottom-of-the-line blender made by Oster available almost anywhere will do just fine and will last a very long time.

2 to 3 servings

2+ cups fresh or frozen blueberries
1+ cup fresh or frozen berry medley
1/2 banana (freeze other half for **Chocolate Frozen Banana Treat**)
1 cup coconut or almond milk
1 1/2 cups **Pomegranate Tea Drink** or real fruit juice mixed 60-70% with water
3 Tbsp. flaxseed meal
2+ cups of fresh loose leaf spinach or kale (NOT optional—trust me, you won't taste it!)

Optional fruits and vegetables: Some of my friends love putting carrots and apples in their smoothies. Use your imagination!

Optional for extra sweetness: 3 or 4 pieces pineapple

If all your ingredients are fresh, throw in a few ice cubes. Blend all the ingredients together in a blender on medium/high speed until thoroughly blended. <u>Best if drunk with a straw!</u> Pour into containers with lids for storage in refrigerator; they can last for two to three days. Take for work and travel—always keep chilled or refrigerated and shake vigorously before drinking. In addition to a great breakfast, this smoothie makes a satisfying snack and can be a frontline defense in the war against sugar cravings.

For extra health:

2 Tbsp. hemp protein powder

1+ cup pomegranate seeds (Almost all stores are now selling fresh pomegranates year-round. They can be terribly messy to deseed; however, I found a green plastic honeycomb device at Walmart for about four dollars that cleanly and easily deseeds them. I really love the sweetness and flavor of these seeds in the smoothies, and they are packed with good nutrition.)

Tasty Mixed Vegetables

Let's face it—the only successful way to eat healthy and lose weight is to eat lots of green and other color vegetables. It is the one common denominator of every food/health expert who has ever written a book or appeared on any cooking and health TV show. But, really, how do you do that when you may not be particularly fond of vegetables? At least as cooked in America, where vegetables are usually over boiled or too lightly steamed and stuck on one-third of a plate only to be pushed around in a desperate attempt to get flavor from other parts of the dish or ultimately disregarded altogether.

I have always thought that sometimes there is "political correctness" applied to vegetables. There was a time when only lightly steamed or very crunchy (close to raw) vegetables were acceptable as healthy and good for you. This is simply not the case. Any level of "doneness" that you like is OK. It is true that you can lose some nutrients when cooking vegetables if you cook them in water. So simply cook them in broth or stock and drink the nutrients later!

I knew one of my first challenges to eating healthy was to learn to like vegetables. Not all of them…

we all have vegetables we detest, and that's fine. Begin work with the ones you already like!

Make a pot of **Super Stock**. (p. 89), chicken or vegetable stock. When boiling, add:

1 cup frozen, <u>shelled</u> edamame (I know I promised nothing exotic, but this is merely the bean from soybeans. It looks like a lima bean but is much firmer in texture. It is loaded with protein and can be found in almost all grocery stores nowadays. Ask for it. Make sure you get the shelled version and not in the pod. Non-GMO is best. If you can't find it, try baby lima beans instead.)

When the stock boils again, add:

2 cups fresh or 1 pkg. frozen French cut green beans OR fresh or frozen green beans cut however you like (I love the skinny ones that are being sold at most grocery stores now in packets. They are very easy to use, just quickly cut off stem end.)

Bring to a boil and simmer for 3–5 minutes. Then add:

As much as you want of any fresh cut broccolini or broccoli or asparagus or cauliflower or Swiss chard or Brussels sprouts or whatever are your favorite green vegetables.

Let simmer for about 5–10 minutes depending on how well you like your vegetables done. **This is important:** Cook the vegetables as long as YOU like them. Some people like them more crunchy and will simmer them less. Others of us like vegetables only when they are thoroughly cooked. Experiment until you get a level of "done-ness" that makes them appealing to YOU.

Now here's the best part! Strain the vegetables, saving the broth in a large glass jar or jars for **Savory Vegetable Soup**. That way you will capture all the nutrients of the vegetables you just cooked instead of throwing them down the drain. Reuse this stock or the soup broth to cook any more vegetables you make during the week—and return the now even more enriched stock back to the jars.

Put the strained vegetables with any **Main Dish** meal (p. 66) you are making. Or mix together with any soup or rice/pasta dish you are cooking to "pump up the volume" and get more nutritious, virtually calorie-free food in your diet. Feel free to mix with a little butter if that's the way you enjoy them. (Remember when you were a kid and butter wasn't akin to poison?) You simply cannot put too much garlic and lemon with vegetables. Sprinkle with **Super Seeds** for extra crunch.

Now here's the second best part! Place the remaining vegetables you don't eat right away in a container(s) for storage in the refrigerator. They will keep for at least five days, which means you do not need to cook vegetables with every meal. Just pull them out of the refrigerator and use them as the primary component of the **Main Dish** meals you make the rest of the week. I have become quite efficient and cook a ton of vegetables on Sunday so I am never without during a busy week.

Tip: Store fresh, raw veggies in "green" bags (available through Amazon.com) when you get home from the grocery store. They really do work to keep your veggies fresher until you can cook them.

Super Seeds (and Nuts)

In large jar mix equal parts:

Raw, unsalted sunflower seeds
Raw, unsalted pumpkin seeds (also known as "pepitas")
Raw slivered or shaved almonds

Shake the jar thoroughly to mix all three together. Sprinkle in virtually everything you make to add extra zing, crunch, and nutrition. Wonderful in salads, with vegetables, and with rice dishes with shrimp, fish, or chicken.

Although this is the basic recipe, feel free to mix in any other raw, unsalted nut that you like – for example – chopped walnuts or cashews.

Perfect Rice Every Time

You don't have to be Asian to cook perfect rice, but cooking this seemingly simple food can cause a lot of frustration. Each type of rice has different cooking times and differing water amounts. If you don't boil or steam it just right, it can be as hard as little rocks or get mushy. And heaven forbid if you don't hear the timer go off! Before I give you a foolproof method to cook rice, let me say a few words about the most common types of rice:

White rice: White rice is processed to remove the bran, which has in it what little nutrition rice has and also most of the fiber. But many people love the taste of white rice. If you like to eat white rice, please buy a quality whole grain type like jasmine or basmati.

Brown rice: This is healthier for you, but some folks don't like its nutty flavor and coarse texture. If that is the case with you, try brown jasmine rice, which is the "smoothest" of the brown rice group. It is my very favorite, and I am never without it in my pantry. I've gotten many of my friends to go half and half with white and brown jasmine, which I think is a good combination until you can transition.

Wild rice: I love wild rice!!!! It has a wonderful texture but also has a distinctive flavor. If I'm making dishes where I don't want the flavor of wild rice to compete with the other flavors—I simply overcook it. Overcooking it by about 10–15 minutes (about an hour total) does little to ruin the texture but for some reason gets rid of a lot of that taste. My standard rice I cook all the time is one-half brown jasmine and one-half wild rice.

OK! So how to not stress about under- or overcooking rice? Put as much rice as you want into a three-quart saucepan with a well-fitting lid. Cover with lots of water, at least double what it calls for in the directions. Bring to a boil and then gently simmer with the lid on—for 5 minutes less than the time called for in the directions to cook the rice. For example, if the directions call for a cooking time of 35 minutes, SET A VERY LOUD TIMER for 30 minutes.

When the timer sounds, with a spoon take a little of the rice and taste test. If it seems almost done or done—excellent! Then take the whole saucepan and the lid over to your sink and tilt the pot at an angle, holding the lid in place just enough to drain all the hot water out. When you think the water is all the way out, shake the pot gently and get even more water out.

Turn OFF the stove burner that you were cooking the rice on and place the pot of rice back on it. Give the pot a little shake to evenly distribute the cooked rice on the bottom of the pot. The rice should still be very hot and steaming. Place the lid slightly ajar enough to let the steam out. Now go away for about 15 minutes.

When you return, your rice will be warm, dry, and perfectly cooked. Fluff lightly with a fork. If not serving then, wait until it cools completely before putting in a container for storing in the refrigerator.

I've found that rice stores well for about four days. When reheating in a microwave, be careful with rice. Better to gently reheat with two or three shorter bursts rather than one long one. Overheating in a microwave will cause rice to explode.

Here's how to make my favorite **combo rice,** which is one-half wild rice and one-half brown jasmine:

1/2 cup wild rice
1/2 cup brown jasmine rice
1 tsp. salt

Put the wild rice in 4 cups of water, bring to a boil and let simmer covered for 25 minutes. Drain water off by holding lid on pot over stove. Put in a new 4 cups of water, the jasmine rice, and salt. Bring to boil and simmer another 25 minutes. Drain all water out over sink, turn off heat, and return pot to burner. Place lid slightly ajar and let pot of rice steam off and cool down for at least 15 minutes. Fluff gently with a fork and serve or refrigerate.

Super Stock

"Stock" or "broth" are fancy terms for the same thing - flavored water that becomes the basis for many recipes. The most standard stock is chicken stock. Foodies take great pride in making it from the leftover bones of a cooked chicken boiled forever with garlic, vegetables such as carrots and celery, and lots of spices. But even expert chefs acknowledge the time-saving advantage of having premade stocks around. Some recommend "broth in a box" chicken, vegetable, or beef, but I think there is a better way to always have stock around.

Why spend all that money on all those broths in a box at the grocery store which are essentially 95% water? You can supply your own water for a whole lot cheaper. They are heavy to carry in from the car and take up a ton of room in your pantry. Make your own quickly with "bouillons," which are concentrated forms of the same flavors that come in boxes. And bouillons allow you to much more precisely control the amount of salt in your food.

It used to be that the most common form of bouillon was tired, salty, dried-out cubes. But now there are much better, more interesting choices. For a long time I've relied on the "Better than Bouillon" brand—which is a very goopy form of bouillon that comes in a jar. The reason I like these is because of the variety of the offerings. When I was going through my vegan phase, their "No Chicken Base" variety was a lifesaver. I still use it to this day instead of real chicken bouillon. In one jar I mix equal parts Low-sodium Vegetable with the No Chicken Base, and I use it with everything. Most grocery stores generally carry the standard vegetable and chicken varieties. But for real fun in the kitchen, go to www.soupsonline.com and see just how many different flavors are offered AND in vegan, organic, or low-sodium varieties. They last a long time in your refrigerator and don't take up much space.

Another variety available at health food stores and online at Amazon.com is the Savory Choice packet bouillon. It is a little more costly for the convenience of little 2 tsp. packets, but they can be excellent for traveling.

Here's my favorite stock/broth recipe—I call it **Super Stock**. All measurements are approximate and to taste:

6 cups water
1 Tbsp. vegetable low-sodium bouillon
1 Tbsp. chicken bouillon (or vegan no chicken)
1 Tbsp. pesto sauce
1 or 2 Tbsp. minced garlic (optional as always)
Juice from one lemon wedge
Dash of hot sauce (optional)

Combine all ingredients and bring to a boil. It can be used right away for **Tasty Mixed Vegetables** (p. 82) or stored in jars in your refrigerator. You can reduce this recipe proportionately when you need small amounts. The usual ratio of bouillon to water is 1 tsp. bouillon to one cup water.

Basic Sauces and Gravies

OK, you are building a mix-and- and match **Main Dish** meal, using 50–60 percent vegetables, perhaps **Tasty Mixed Vegetables**, already made and stored in the refrigerator. To that you have added some **Perfect Rice Every Time** also already made and stored in the refrigerator, and some fresh or leftover sautéed or broiled chicken, fish, or shrimp or even some grass-fed ground beef. For a vegetarian option, you can add tofu or a portion of an Amy's entre such as Bean or Cheese Enchiladas or Gluten-free Lasagna, and so forth. Use your imagination!!!

But to bring the whole meal together, you might want to add a wonderful, flavorful, easy-to-make **sauce or gravy** that's only thirty to forty calories and fat free! Here's how you do it:

2 Servings

In a smallish glass mixing jar, add:

1/2 cup cold water and

1/2 cup milk or milk substitute (any kind of "milk," dairy 2%, coconut, almond are all OK depending on how creamy you want texture)

2 Tbsp. **gravy packet** - type and flavor of your choice (see below) – generally chosen based on the meat you are cooking

Optional: Any seasonings you would like (ie. garlic, Italian herb, pesto, tarragon)

Shake the jar well until the powder from the gravy packet is dissolved. Use a spoon or small spatula to make sure any left on the bottom is dissolved.

Heat a small skillet to medium heat. Pour mixture from jar into hot skillet. Stir immediately and continuously until sauce comes to a boil. Turn off heat. If too thick, add a little water or white wine. Pour over all of your already heated-up items in your **Main Dish** meal. If you've made too much gravy, return to glass jar and store in the refrigerator and use for tomorrow's lunch. Brilliant! Will last for up to five days.

Commercial Gravy Packet Options

Acceptable: Knorr brand or McCormick brand packets are found in almost all grocery stores and Walmart. These have great flavor but contain small amounts of wheat flour and other additives and are saltier. It's not enough wheat flour to trigger cravings, I think, but if you are shooting for gluten free—skip these and move on to the next option. **Best flavors:** Depending on your meat item, enjoy roasted chicken, herb beef, and garlic and herb (yummy with fish!!!). International flavors are fun too.

Much healthier: In health food stores you will find cornstarch- or rice flour–based gravy packets made without meat, but the way they make them mimics meat flavors. I LOVE THESE and use them with everything! **Hain** makes a great brown gravy packet.

Road's End Organics makes a wonderful savory herb that works over almost anything, especially fish and chicken. Poke around this little section of the store, and you will find all sorts of gravy packets that are wheat free, organic, fat free, low calorie, and meat free with wonderful exotic flavors you will be curious to experiment with.

Or Make Your Own Gravy:

1/2 cup milk or nondairy milk
1/2 cup cool water
2 tsp. cornstarch (organic, non-GMO would be great)
1 tsp. chicken, beef, or vegetable bouillon—low-sodium best

Optional:

2 tsp. pesto sauce
1 Tbsp. minced garlic
2 Tbsp. fresh salsa
Juice from 1 large lemon wedge

Put all ingredients in a jar and shake until they are mixed thoroughly. Pour into a hot, small skillet and stir constantly until mixture just starts to boil. Remove from heat and stir for a minute longer. Salt and pepper to taste.

Savory Vegetable Soup

~~~~~~

Having jars of a flavorful, nutritious soup around all the time is a great way to beat the "I'm opening the refrigerator and can't figure out what to eat...." blues. Before you get into real trouble, pour yourself a mug of this, maybe add some veggies or rice – and if you are in a particularly decadent mood – sprinkle with some cheese. Making this soup is a way to get rid of all those chopped trimmings from the increased level of vegetables you are now eating and all the veggies that have gotten a little old to eat raw but are still perfectly good for soup. You will still be throwing them away at the end, but at least you've squeezed every last bit of nutrition out of them!

To a big pot of **Super Stock** you have strained from making **Tasty Mixed Vegetables**, add:

All trimmings cut from raw veggies for **Tasty Mixed Vegetables**
One thinly sliced large yellow onion
5–10 green onions, sliced
More minced garlic (In my opinion, the more garlic the better!!!)
1/4 cup fresh salsa
Dash hot sauce

Any vegetables in your refrigerator that are past their prime but not spoiled—for example, carrots, celery, mushrooms (use this as an opportunity to clean out your refrigerator of older vegetables before shopping for new ones)

Optional: Get Creative!

Fresh parsley
Fresh cilantro
One dried Ancho chili pepper, deseeded and washed (gives broth
    a warm, smoky flavor without too much heat)
Turmeric
More pesto sauce
More lemon, squeezed
Dried lentils—throw in 1/4 cup for a smoky flavor and heartier
    consistency

Cut up vegetables into pieces or slices. Put in a large pot with the **Super Stock**. You may need to add additional water to barely cover all the raw vegetables. Bring to a boil and simmer for over an hour. Pour and strain the liquid through a large, fine metal strainer into another pot and push gently with the back of a big spoon to get all the liquid out of the cooked vegetable mix. Discard what remains of the cooked vegetables. (Think of throwing away the bones from turkey soup made the day after Thanksgiving.) Pour remaining soup stock into jars for storage in refrigerator. Use a large mouth funnel if necessary to prevent mess.

Together with a **Basic Berry Smoothie**, drinking a mug of this soup in the morning makes a great healthy breakfast for those who know eating breakfast is good for you but just can't deal with solid food early in the morning. This will fill you up and easily carry you to lunch.

Also makes a great afternoon snack on a cold day.

Anytime during the week you are making vegetables, you can heat up this soup/stock to cook them in. Return soup to jars and put back in the refrigerator. It will flavor the vegetables, and you won't lose any of the nutrients of the newly cooked vegetables!

This is an excellent place to add a tablespoon or two of **hemp protein powder** for extra protein.

Chicken Quesadilla and Bean Soup

This is a hearty main dish soup that is a delicious treat when you are in the mood for something spicy and Latin.

3 to 4 servings

Soup

4 cups chicken or vegetable stock or **Super Stock**
1/2 cup chopped or thinly sliced yellow onion
3 Tbsp. minced garlic
1/4 cup fresh salsa
1/2 can green enchilada sauce
1/2 cup chopped cilantro (optional)
8- to 12-ounce chicken (already cooked, or brown raw pieces for
     5 minutes on each side then simmer for 45 minutes in soup itself)
1 can drained beans of your choice (garbanzo, red, pinto, black all
    work nicely)

Cook all ingredients together for 10–15 minutes.

Quesadillas (one per person)

2 corn tortillas per person

1/4 cup shredded cheese (mozzarella, white cheddar, or pepper
    jack are fine)

Put a little olive oil in a pan. Heat both sides of the tortillas, flipping them with a spatula or by hand. When heated through, sprinkle the cheese evenly over one tortilla and place another tortilla on top of it and press with a spatula. Flip and grill both sides like a skinny grilled cheese sandwich. When the cheese is thoroughly melted, remove from heat and cut into strips or bite-sized pieces. Add to soup just before serving. Add dashes of hot sauce of your choice to taste.

Alternatives: Any kind of meat will work in this soup—with grass-fed hamburger it becomes a taco soup!

For extra health: Here is a great place to "pump up the volume" with vegetables. Some very finely sliced cabbage and celery would be a welcome addition.

Three-Bean Lentil Soup

This is a hearty, flexible, "everything but the kitchen sink" type of soup that can be made several different ways. The reason I use lentils as the base is because they have a unique, smoky flavor all their own, which makes them compatible with—and different from—every other type of bean.

4 servings

4 cups chicken or vegetable stock or **Super Stock**
1/2 cup chopped celery
1/2 cup chopped green or yellow onion
2 Tbsp. minced garlic
1 cup lentils
1 cup frozen shelled edamame (or baby lima beans)
1 cup canned/cooked garbanzo beans, or red beans, or pinto beans
     (any type of bean you want!)

In a three-quart stockpot, gently sauté onion and celery for a few minutes in olive oil. Add stock. Rinse dried lentils thoroughly in a fine metal strainer and add to pot. Bring to a boil, cover, and reduce heat to low and gently simmer for one hour.

After an hour—add edamame and other bean(s). Cook for another 20–30 minutes, and then it is ready to serve. When thoroughly cooled, this soup can be put in plastic containers and frozen for use another day.

Options: If you are having a noodle craving—at the same time you put in the edamame, you can put in some Asian rice noodles; they will cook easily in 20 minutes. Ham or sausages from pasture-raised pork without nitrates would make this a hearty main dish when served over rice and vegetables.

For extra health: Put in some chopped kale, spinach, or Swiss chard at the 20-minute mark.

Diana's Deviled Egg Spread

Boil 4 free-range eggs until hard-boiled, then refrigerate for at least 3 hours.

Peel the eggs, cut in half, and separate the yolks from the white. In a small mixing bowl, mash the yolks gently with a fork, adding:

3 Tbsp. of your favorite mayonnaise (check out organic and olive oil)
2 Tbsp. mustard
Salt, pepper, and paprika to taste
1 tsp. dill relish (optional)

Once that's all thoroughly mixed together, add:

2 chopped egg whites from the previously peeled, cooked eggs
2 celery stalks, inner whiter stalks sliced/chopped finely
2 green onions, white ends sliced/chopped very finely

Stir with fork until all mixed together well. Refrigerate to allow flavors to blend.

Essentially you have "pumped up the volume" of the yolk mixture with the virtually no-calorie, no-carb egg whites and veggies. This is an excellent spread on celery sticks, with (no-wheat) crackers, used as a mushroom stuffer, and so on. You can even stuff the remaining egg white halves for a more traditional treat similar to Deviled Eggs.

When you finish with the mixture, you may look at it and say, "Why, this is just a fancy version of old-fashioned egg salad!" Ah, yes, but would you have been nearly as interested in it if I had called it "Egg Salad Sandwhich Dip"? I think not!

Salads and Dressings

I have had a love/hate relationship with salads for years. There are times when I like them, primarily in the summer, and there are times when eating them seemed like either a consolation prize or a punishment. The lowest point in my relationship with salads was when I was on some sort of diet and I felt the only thing I could eat when going out to a restaurant was a salad. Like vegetables, when I undertook my new healthy eating style, I decided to reignite my love of salads no matter what it took.

Salad Dressings

When I really thought about it, it wasn't so much the salad that bothered me—it was the lousy choices of salad dressings I thought I had to make. I loved ranch and blue cheese, but it been pounded into me these were too high in fat, too rich, and too creamy. For me, most oil and vinaigrette dressings were way too sour or bitter, and I just hated them. And to me, the low-fat versions of any salad dressing tasted completely off-key—lifeless copies of the real thing.

If you have a low-fat healthy dressing you love – that is fantastic and please keep using it. But I had to come to grips with the fact I really only enjoy salads if I use tastier, creamier salad dressings. **Then good news!** I heard about Bolthouse Yogurt Dressings, which were only forty-five calories for two tablespoons. In and of themselves, the dressings didn't wow me. But mixed half and half with their higher-fat counterpart and some Greek yogurt—they were delicious. And I was able to cut the fat and the calories of the richer dressing almost in half when averaged out.

So I use Bolthouse yogurt classic ranch combined with Greek yogurt as the base for all my dressings. Customized variations include:

Thousand Island

1/2 cup Bolthouse yogurt classic ranch dressing / Greek yogurt
1/4 cup ketchup (without added sugar is best)
2 Tbsp. dill relish (not sweet relish!)

Chipotle Ranch

In equal parts, mix Bolthouse yogurt classic ranch dressing with any chipotle dressing you like. One of my favorites is the Marketside brand creamy chipotle ranch yogurt dressing sold at Walmart.

Blue Cheese

1/2 cup Bolthouse yogurt classic ranch / Greek yogurt
1/2 cup blue cheese or gorgonzola crumble (goat cheese is great too)
2 Tbsp. sour cream (optional)

Lightly mash all ingredients together. Salt and pepper to taste

Anyway—you get the point. By making your own simple dressings like this, you not only cut calories, but you can customize them by adding lemon juice, hot sauce, pesto sauce, smashed avocado for a Green Goddess variation...use your imagination! Make a lot at one time so you don't have to do it each time you make a salad.

Healthier Choice: The goal is eventually transition to Greek yogurt which is really good for you and has far fewer added ingredients than the Bolthouse brand. I would start mixing in the Greek yogurt in greater and greater quantities as your taste buds adjust.

Tip: Don't forget to take a little single serving jar of your favorite dressing with you when you travel or go out to dinner in case you have no other acceptable option other than a salad.

The Actual Salad

Here is where I don't insult your intelligence by suggesting to you what to put in your salad. Any woman over twenty years old knows what salad ingredients she likes and what she dislikes. But just for fun, I will tell you what I like in mine:

Lettuce (generally organic romaine, but I will admit to a fondness
      for iceberg)
Bean sprouts
Hard-boiled egg
1/4 cup fresh salsa (I'm too lazy to chop onions and tomatoes each time)

Cooked shrimp or salmon or canned tuna

Super Seeds sprinkled on top

Optional if I have around:

Garbanzo beans (sometimes known as chickpeas)
Hearts of palm
Avocado

Not that I believe in counting calories, but the salad ingredients total about 100 and the dressing about 100, which I consider a deal for that much flavor and nutrition!

Egg Foo Young

~~~~~~~~

The wonderful thing about this quick and easy Asian dish is that it can be served for breakfast, lunch, or dinner. If you think Asian cooking is difficult and out of your league, think again!

2 servings

2 free-range eggs
1 1/2 cups fresh bean sprouts
1/2 cup fresh or frozen smaller shrimp
2 Tbsp. thinly sliced green onion

Sauté shrimp and green onion in a 9–10" pan for about 5 minutes or until shrimp is cooked through. Add bean sprouts and stir until bean sprouts have just started to heat through, about 2 minutes. Whisk the eggs and then pour into pan. Distribute egg mixture throughout the pan as the items all cook together. When egg has cooked on one side (be careful not to burn), flip the whole thing over to cook on the other side. You may need to cut it in half to turn with spatula. This thick "pancake" is done when the egg is cooked completely through. Serve over heated rice (optional) and pour **Chinese Gravy** over the whole thing.

Chinese Gravy

In a small mixing jar, mix together:

1/2 cup cool water
1 1/2 tsp. cornstarch
2 tsp. low-sodium organic tamari sauce
Dash hot sauce (optional)

Shake jar until all items are thoroughly mixed together, making sure cornstarch is not stuck on the bottom. Immediately pour into a small pan that has already been heated to high. Stir constantly until the gravy turns translucent and just starts to boil, then quickly remove from heat. Pour over cooked **Egg Foo Young**.

Cheesy Brussels Sprouts

Think you have to give up all comfort food if you are eating healthy? Think again! But please keep in mind this is **not** an everyday dish.....

1 serving

Brussels Sprouts

3 cups Brussels sprouts, bases removed and sliced into 1/4" pieces
     or
2 cups Brussels sprouts and 1 cup cauliflower
     or
Any amount of any green vegetable you REALLY like

Bring some **Super Stock** or water to a boil. Add Brussels sprouts and simmer for 20 minutes. Drain. If using **Super Stock**, strain back into jar and refrigerate.

Drizzle low-sodium tamari (or soy) sauce and garlic powder on the warm Brussels sprouts.

Mac and Cheese

1 pkg. Amy's **gluten-free** macaroni and cheese (Blue plaid on the box/label – not the Green plaid!)

Microwave for about 4 minutes. It won't be quite done and will be goopy. Put half of package in a container and refrigerate for later. Take the other half and pour onto nonstick tin foil in a small, shallow baking pan. Place in toaster oven or top rack of oven set on "broil" for about 10–15 minutes or until top has started to get nice and brown.

Put the now nicely browned mac and cheese in with the warm Brussels sprouts and toss. Heat up in microwave if necessary. Enjoy...only 200 calories for a delicious treat.

Steamed Artichokes

Steamed artichokes can make a fabulous low-calorie snack or appetizer. But they take a long time (1–2 hours) to cook properly. This is a project for a rainy day while you're spending most of your time curled up with a good book.

2 artichokes
Between 1 to 2 cups chicken or vegetable stock or **Super Stock**

Wash artichokes thoroughly. Trim bottom stem to about 1/2 to 1 inch below artichoke base. Place in a large stock pot with secure lid. They can rest gently at an angle where they naturally lie without propping up.

Place 2 inches of stock on the bottom and bring to a boil. Reduce heat, cover, and simmer for 30 minutes. Then check on the pot and replace any liquid that has steamed off. With tongs, rotate the artichokes around completely so the opposite side is now in the liquid. Bring stock back to a boil, reduce heat to a low simmer, and steam for another 30 minutes

After an hour, check on artichokes. Take two forks with their tines upside down and gently pull the leaves apart at the top, just enough to separate all the leaves a little. Now take a turkey baster and draw in some of the stock and bathe the artichokes in the broth. Repeat several times until the artichokes have had broth squirted all throughout them, particularly in the center where the heart is. Bring stock back to a boil, reduce heat, and simmer for another 30 minutes.

After an hour and a half total cooking time, test the artichoke to see if a middle leaf will separate from the artichoke with almost no pressure. If it takes any tugging whatsoever, return to broth for steaming another 20–30 minutes. The leaves should virtually fall off the artichoke when properly cooked.

When done, remove artichoke with tongs and drain above pot upside down. Let cool to room temperature before eating by separating the leaves and dipping in mayonnaise or butter. The artichoke you don't eat should be thoroughly wrapped in tin foil and refrigerated. I will last up to four days in the refrigerator.

Vegetable and Potato Frittata

"Frittata" is a fancy Mediterranean name for a very thick egg-and-potato pancake. This is a great brunch or anytime dish to make when you have a leftover baked potato in the refrigerator.

2 servings

3 free-range eggs
1/2 already baked potato, with skin on is great
1 cup **Tasty Mixed Vegetables**, cooked asparagus or broccoli
2 Tbsp. thinly sliced green or yellow onion

Cut the potato and vegetables into bite-sized pieces. In a 9–10" frying pan, sauté the onion, potato, and vegetables in a little olive oil until heated through. Scramble the eggs and add to pan, distributing evenly. Cook on one side and then gently flip over. Cook until egg is completely cooked and then serve. If you don't like the pancake idea, just make into a hash-type scramble. If you want some meat in the dish, pasture-raised ham would work well. You could sprinkle with a little grated cheese on top

Salt and pepper to taste.

Mistaken Identity Mashed Potatoes

OK, OK—I get it, you are really tired of rice. How about some mashed potatoes without all the starch and carbs? Cauliflower mashed potatoes are nothing new, and I certainly can't take credit for the fantastic idea of swapping out potatoes for cauliflower. But the problem with most recipes I've found is that they add enormous amounts of butter, milk, or cream (saturated dairy fat) or even— EGADS!—cream cheese to give them the creamy consistency and flavor. All you are doing then is swapping out the bad starch and carbs in potatoes for a bunch of almost as bad saturated dairy fat. I think this is a good alternative that adds protein. My Southern girlfriend Sandy paid me the ultimate compliment—she said she could serve them to her meat and potatoes lovin' husband and he wouldn't know the difference!

2 to 3 servings

1 medium head cauliflower
1/3 cup canned or cooked large butter beans (I like Bush's brand best)
1 tsp. butter
Salt and pepper to taste

Cut the cauliflower florets from the stem and then grate them with a cheese grater. The grated cauliflower will look like pebbles, and a medium head of cauliflower should grate enough pebbles for about 3 cups. Put the cauliflower pebbles into gently boiling, salted water and cook for 30 minutes.

Drain the cooked cauliflower through a **fine** metal strainer. Push with the back of a large serving spoon to get as much liquid out as possible. Lift and push again. Don't worry! You won't push the cauliflower through. Add the butter beans and mash together. Transfer to a food processer (mini-chopper is fine), add butter, and "whip," or blend on medium or high, until the cauliflower is no longer grainy to taste. This mixture should be creamy in texture and have the same consistency, or stiffness, as real mashed potatoes.

Salt and pepper to taste and serve. Any remaining portions can be refrigerated for a few days and added to **Main Dish** meals when reheated.

Additional tips: If you like garlic mashed potatoes, add some minced or roasted garlic to the mixture before you blend it in the food processor. Thin sliced green onions cooked together with the cauliflower pebbles can be tasty too.

Do not throw the stem, also known as the heart, from the cauliflower away. Cut off the green leaves at the base and, with a sharp paring knife, cut the heart into thin slices. These make great no-calorie "chips" with which to eat **Diana's Deviled Egg Spread** or hummus.

Killer Chicken with Pan Gravy

It seems like for eons the go-to staple of the diet world has been a chicken breast with some vegetables and a little rice for dinner. BORING! Not to mention it can taste like cardboard and doesn't satisfy very well. This recipe, in particular with the alternative seasoning combinations at the bottom, is the "little black dress" of dinner meals. It is only about thirty extra calories for the sauce, which makes ALL the difference. It is super simple once you've done it a couple of times and will please your family too.

2 servings

2 or 3 free-range chicken pieces—light or dark
2 tsp. low-sodium tamari sauce
2 Tbsp. minced garlic
1/2 small yellow onion
2 Tbsp. chicken gravy packet

Sparingly coat chicken with tamari sauce and 2 tbsp. garlic and punch a bunch of holes with a fork into the chicken to tenderize it. Refrigerate for at least half an hour or up to one day. This marinated chicken can also be used for **Stupendous Stir-Fry** (p. 126) by slicing it paper thin on the diagonal.

When ready to cook—heat up a pan (you want the pan to fit the pieces) with a little olive or coconut oil. Brown the chicken pieces about 3 minutes each side. Just before finishing browning, you could add the thinly sliced yellow or green onions to lightly sauté.

When done browning the chicken, put about 1 inch of **Savory Vegetable Soup** (p. 94) or **Super Stock** or any available chicken broth in pan. Do not completely cover chicken with soup/stock/broth—that's a whole different recipe. Stir gently so all ingredients combine and fried bits are loosened from the bottom of the pan. Cover and simmer for about 45 minutes, checking every once in a while to make sure stock never falls below 1/2 inch in the pan (if it does, just add **water**, not more stock)) and that chicken pieces are not sticking to bottom. About halfway through, flip the chicken over. Chicken is done when it comes apart easily when prodded with a fork.

Mix 2 Tbsp. of a chicken gravy packet with 1/3 cup cold water or milk in a small jar, and stir or shake to dissolve thoroughly. Add to chicken and broth and bring to a boil, stirring constantly. Turn off heat and let sit a few minutes.

Serve over lots of **Tasty Mixed Vegetables** and **Perfect Rice Every Time** and/or **Mistaken Identity Mashed Potatoes**.

Optional flavorings to add while chicken is simmering:

Pesto sauce and lemon for chicken pesto

Green enchilada sauce and fresh salsa for chicken verde—spice up with hot sauce

Organic spaghetti sauce and mushrooms for chicken cacciatore

Curry powder, cumin, and turmeric for chicken curry—very exotic!

Dried tarragon and lemon and white wine for chicken tarragon - very romantic!

Turkey à la King

This is an old-fashioned dish that helps out when you think you are in a chicken rut!

2 servings

In a mixing jar with a tight fitting lid, put:

1 turkey or chicken gravy packet (see p. 92)
1 Tbsp. cornstarch
1 Tbsp. coconut flour
1/2 cup coconut milk
1/2 cup cool water

Put the lid on the jar and shake thoroughly two or three times. Put mixture in a saucepan at medium heat, **stirring constantly**. Using a whisk can be helpful. Bring just to a boil and then turn off heat. Keep stirring sauce until it no longer thickens. If the sauce is too thick, whisk in some chicken stock, coconut milk, or water. Salt and pepper to taste.

To the sauce add:

2 cups cooked turkey, cut up or shredded in pieces
1 cup cooked carrots
1 cup cooked peas
1 cup of a lightly sautéed mix of diced onions and celery

Stir all together for about 5 minutes over medium heat to combine all flavors.

Serve over a shallow bowl of heated **Perfect Rice Every Time** and **Tasty Mixed Vegetables**. Sprinkle with **Super Seeds** for a little extra crunch.

Sparkling Shrimp (or Sparkling Salmon, Swordfish, Sea Bass, or Tilapia)

This is an easy, quick, delicious dish that makes an extra special jazzy something to serve when company comes over. The components are simple and classic, but the sauce adds a gourmet touch that will make everyone's mouth "sparkle"! Shrimp is a treat for everyone, and this recipe contains no wheat, flour, or dairy and does not have all the fat (oil and butter) of a traditional scampi dish.

2 servings

10 jumbo or 15 large fresh or frozen peeled, deveined shrimp
Low-sodium tamari or soy sauce
Olive oil
1 Tbsp. minced garlic
1 or 2 green onions, finely chopped
1 cup sliced mushrooms (I love the small brownish Baby Bella
    mushrooms)

Sparkling Sauce

1/3 cup dairy or nondairy milk
3/4 cup water (cool)

2 tsp. cornstarch
1/2 tsp. chicken (or vegetable) bouillon—low-sodium good
2 tsp. pesto sauce
1 Tbsp. minced garlic
2 Tbsp. fresh salsa
Juice from 1 large lemon wedge

In a medium-sized mixing jar, add all ingredients for the sauce. Shake thoroughly until all ingredients are dissolved in jar. Bring a medium-sized (9–10") pan to hot and add contents of jar. Stir for a minute or two until sauce becomes slightly translucent, thickens, and begins to boil. Turn off heat and set aside.

In a large skillet, heat some olive oil. Place shrimp in pan, reduce heat to medium, and drizzle with tamari sauce and cook for only a minute or two a side for fresh shrimp, longer for frozen shrimp. Add green onions and mushrooms and finish sautéing with shrimp. Add a little water or stock if necessary to keep pan from burning. **Note:** It is really easy to overcook shrimp and really hard to undercook it. It is done when solidly white throughout.

When shrimp is finished, add the sauce that is in the other pan and stir all together for 1 minute. At this point I would splash in some white wine—but of course this is optional!

Heat up plates with generous servings of any kind of fresh vegetable or **Tasty Mixed Vegetables** and **Perfect Rice Every Time** that you already have made up or have in your refrigerator. Add shrimp mixture to plate, nestled on top of rice and vegetables. Spoon sauce over everything. Sprinkle with **Super Seeds** and serve.

Added bonus: This sauce can work equally as well with nice pieces of a dense seafood such as salmon, sea bass, tilapia, or swordfish. Just broil or sauté the fish separately with drizzles of tamari sauce and lemon and put on top of vegetables and rice and pour sauce over all. It also works as a light, zingy sauce with cooked chicken breasts.

Troubleshooting: If the sauce is too thick, add water or white wine in small splashes until it reaches the desired consistency. If too thin, gently steam or boil off excess water. If too salty, add more lemon and a splash of white wine. If not salty enough, add dashes of low-sodium tamari (or soy) to taste.

Salmon or Crab Cakes

These make a great snack, light meal, or interesting salad topper. They refrigerate well and can be warmed up in the microwave.

Makes about 4 cakes

First, assemble the dry ingredients for the coating mixture and set aside:

1 cup flaxseed meal
1 Tbsp. Italian seasonings
1 tsp. garlic powder
1 tsp. salt

Gently sauté some thinly sliced green onion and celery in olive or coconut oil or a little chicken stock until softened.

In a separate bowl, put:

1 whisked raw egg
1/2 cup green onion and celery mixture
2 cups loose cooked salmon or crab meat (can be canned or fresh)
2 Tbsp. coconut flour
1/2 cup shredded mozzarella cheese
2 Tbsp. dill pickle relish (NOT sweet relish)
1 tsp. garlic powder

Mix all together with your hand, like you were making a meatloaf. Divide into four balls and then gently pat down to form 1-inch thick patties. Coat both sides liberally with coating mixture pressing it lightly into the cakes.

Heat a pan to medium/high and melt 2 tbsp. of coconut oil. When hot, gently lift fish patties with a spatula and place in pan. Cook for 7–10 minutes or until crispy. It may be necessary to add a little more coconut oil as the patties cook to keep them from sticking. Use as much as you think necessary but as little as possible. When one side is done, GENTLY lift up with spatula and fry other side 5–7 minutes or until crispy. Be careful when turning over so that the patty sticks together. If it doesn't, mush it back together in the pan. Remove from heat and cool before serving.

Healthy Beef Stroganoff

When you really want to indulge, this dish will do the trick! Hard to believe you can eat like this and still call it healthy...

2 servings

8 oz. grass-fed beef sirloin, rib eye cut, skirt steak cut **or** ground beef
2 packets brown gravy (see **Basic Sauces and Gravies** p. 91)
1/4 cup thinly sliced yellow onion
1 tsp. garlic powder
1 cup sliced fresh mushrooms
1/4 cup sour cream

Take the sour cream out of the refrigerator and let it come to room temperature (about 20 minutes).

Holding a very sharp knife at a diagonal angle, slice the beef into very thin slices—much like you would if you were making it for stir-fry. Heat a 9–10" frying pan to medium/high heat and lay the beef slices flat into the pan and drizzle with a little low-sodium tamari sauce and the garlic powder. Sauté the beef about 3 minutes each side and then sauté the onions until translucent. It may be necessary to add a little olive oil or coconut oil if beef or onions start sticking. If using ground beef, sauté in bite-sized pieces.

In a mixing jar, mix the gravy packets with cool water per directions on the packet. Shake well. Pour into beef/onion and stir until gravy has thickened and is just about to boil. Add mushrooms and turn burner to almost off.

Place the sour cream it in a bowl and gradually stir in a spoonful of the beef gravy. When that is absorbed, stir in another spoonful of the gravy. Then very gradually add the sour cream to the pan with the beef and mushrooms. If you do not do this process of gradually raising the temperature of the sour cream, it will curdle on you as soon as it hits the hot beef and gravy mixture.

Reheat and stir everything together for a few minutes. Salt and pepper to taste. I add a couple of dashes of hot sauce for little zing. Serve over heated **Perfect Rice Every Time** and **Tasty Mixed Vegetables**.

Stupendous Stir-Fry

The trick to making great stir-fry is to realize that not all the vegetables require the same amount of cooking time. The cooking of the vegetables needs to be layered in time so they are all cooked to perfection at the end. This may seem like one of the most complicated recipes in the book—but if you practice it a few times, you can become an expert at making this incredibly healthy masterpiece in no time.

1-2 servings

Vegetables

Stage 1 Possibilities

Celery
Green onion
Bok choy (baby is fine)
Snow peas
Broccoli (broccolini is best)
Asparagus
Fresh snap peas
Edamame

Stage 2

Water chestnuts, sliced

Bean or sunflower sprouts
Sliced cabbage (optional)

Meat (definitely optional)

2 or 3 oz. per person of **paper-thin, sliced** on the diagonal grass-fed beef, free-range chicken, or pasture-raised pork. Whole shrimp or tofu can be used too.

Chinese Gravy

1/2 cup cold water
2 tsp. low-sodium tamari sauce
1 1/2 tsp. cornstarch
Dash hot sauce

Cooking Instructions

It is best when making stir-fry to have all ingredients ready before actually starting to cook. In a small skillet, place about 2 cups of stage 1 vegetables of your choice in an inch of water. Bring to a boil, then turn off heat and leave vegetables to blanch for about 10 minutes.

Stir all ingredients for the **Chinese Gravy** together in a small jar and set aside.

OK! Heat up a 10" frying pan, no wok needed. Melt 1 tsp. coconut oil. When heated to high, gently layer in the very thin pieces of sliced meat (or whole shrimp). Drizzle with some tamari sauce and sprinkle with garlic powder. When brown on one side, turn pieces over, brown on the other side, and push meat to one side of skillet.

Drain blanched stage 1 vegetables until all almost all of the water is gone. Put into the hot skillet and stir gently to heat up thoroughly. Stir in meat pieces from side of skillet. Stir in stage 2 vegetables. Stir gravy **in jar** one last time and pour into hot vegetables and meat. Keep stirring (about 2 minutes) until all ingredients are really hot and gravy/sauce has turned thicker and translucent. Remove from heat.

In a shallow bowl heat some cooked rice (white or brown jasmine is best, and leftover rice is fine!) in microwave for about 30 seconds. Pour stir-fry over rice and top with **Super Seeds** for crunch. You might need a little more tamari sauce to taste and, if you like, more hot sauce to spice things up. Maybe even a little minced ginger? A few cashews?

Enjoy! This is a really low-fat, low-carb but very filling meal with tons of deliciously flavored vegetables. If you cut up the stage 1 vegetables ahead of time (I have a container filled with three meals' worth)—it really doesn't take that much time to cook. It may take a few tries to get it just right, but don't get discouraged. In no time you'll be turning out better (and healthier) stir-fry than the local Chinese joint!

Amazing Pizza Crust

I debated about putting this recipe in the book. It is neither quick nor easy and will require a few items to make that you generally might not have around. I had to go out and buy an old-fashioned rolling pin, cheesecloth, and parchment paper (I am definitely NOT a baker!). It is a little time-consuming and messy but once you've made it a few times it gets much easier. My friends insisted I include this recipe because, when properly made, it really can taste like and has the texture of a wonderful herbed Mediterranean-style flatbread. And better still—it has no wheat and almost no carbs. If you dare, check it out and Good Luck!

1 medium-sized crust

4 cups grated cauliflower florets (see **Mistaken Identity Mashed Potatoes** p. 113)

Combine following dry ingredients together in a small bowl:

3 Tbsp. coconut flour
2 Tbsp. flaxseed meal
1 tsp. baking soda
1 tsp. baking powder
1 tsp. salt
1 tsp. Italian-style herbs (optional)
1 tsp. garlic powder (optional)

2 egg whites and 1 egg yolk (raw, whisked together)
1/3 cup shredded skim milk mozzarella cheese

Preheat oven to 400 degrees. Boil the grated cauliflower "sand pebbles" in salted water for 30 minutes. Drain as much water as you can out of them by straining with a **fine** metal strainer and pressing with the back of a large spoon. Then cool. Put the cauliflower mush in a cheesecloth or kitchen towel and twist it down into a ball, straining even more water out of the cauliflower. Put the now as-dry-as-possible cauliflower mush into a bowl.

Add dry ingredients. Add egg and cheese. Put your hands in and mix it all together thoroughly as you would a meatloaf. Form into a tight, round ball and place on a large piece of lightly greased (olive oil or butter) parchment paper. Put another piece of parchment paper on top and begin gently rolling both ways with a rolling pin. The "dough" will slowly roll out into a circle or an oblong shape. Roll until dough is about three-quarters of an inch thick. Remove top parchment paper and discard. If the edge has frayed, push back together with palm of your hand.

Place dough—still on parchment paper—on a cookie sheet and bake in the oven at 400 degrees for 30 minutes. Gently turn over and bake for another 10 minutes.* The resulting "bread" should be crisp on the outside and have a bread-like center. Cool a little before serving.

This flatbread can be cut in pieces and frozen. Then you can take out, defrost, and reheat and crisp back up in a toaster. You can even put a little **Diana's Deviled Egg Spread** (p.) in between two pieces and have an egg salad sandwich!

For extra health:

1 Tbsp. hemp protein powder

1 Tbsp. nutritional yeast

* If you want to make pizza, it would be at this point to add your toppings and put it back in for the remaining 10 minutes.

Dreamy Dark Chocolate Sauce

In a small mixing jar, put:

1/3 cup coconut or almond milk
2 Tbsp. dark chocolate 100% cocoa powder (I like Hershey's
Special which is found almost everywhere)

Stir or shake thoroughly until the powder is completely absorbed,
then add:

2 Tbsp. (or to taste) raw, unprocessed organic honey. It helps to
warm the honey in a microwave for 10–15 seconds to make
it runny and easier to mix.

Stir this mixture well and then close the jar and shake. Refrigerate.
Will last for at least a week. Every time you take it out, stir or
shake again. Absolutely fabulous for dunking fresh or frozen fruit
(i.e., strawberries...YUM!).

Chocolate Frozen Banana Treat

Peel 1 banana. Cut off tips at each end. Cut in half and skewer each half and with a stick. Skinny, round popsicle sticks (Walmart in party section) work well, or try children's chopsticks, which are more festive and reusable. I used the handle end of plastic spoons until I could find the right thing. Freeze the skewered halves for at least 3 hours in a zip-top baggie in the freezer. They will last for about a week.

When ready to eat, take out one half and place it on a small plate or small shallow bowl. Shake the jar with the **Dreamy Dark Chocolate Sauce** and drizzle two spoonfuls all over the banana. Then, if you like, top the banana with low-fat whipped cream, approximately 3 tablespoons. Sprinkle with finely chopped walnut pieces.

Holding the banana by the stick, twirl it slowly in the chocolate, whipped cream, and nut conglomeration and savor slowly. This comes in at about 100 calories and satisfies like Ben & Jerry's Chunky Monkey ice cream! If you don't want to bother with the popsicle stick, just take the frozen banana pieces and mash them in a bowl with the chocolate sauce and walnuts. As it defrosts a little, it will have a consistency very much like ice cream. Or whip up a little bit more in your mini-food processor. You can experiment with other types of nuts and nut butters to find the combination you like best.

Fruit Cobbler

1 cup frozen or fresh fruit of your choice (frozen peaches are wonderful in this)
3 Tbsp. chopped walnuts
1 tsp. cinnamon
1/4 tsp. vanilla
Light whipped cream (organic if you can find it)
Raisins

If frozen, unthaw the fruit and keep covered in refrigerator until ready
to eat. Cut up fruit into bite-sized pieces. Warm slightly. Add cinnamon and vanilla.

Sprinkle with walnuts. Lightly cover with whipped cream, top
with a sprinkle of raisins and enjoy!

18
My Favorite Health and Food Gurus

~~~~~~

Before I embarked on this or any other healthy eating plan, I wanted to learn all I could from people who really are the experts. So I read and read, viewed many specials on PBS, and spent hours on Google. I have never stopped learning and will never stop as there is new information coming out all the time.

After all the hours of research...here are the folks whose advice I have come to rely on the most in designing my recipes:

Dr. V. J. Vad, *Stop Pain*: I saw Dr. Vad on a PBS special and it literally changed my life. For the first time I saw the relationship between pain (inflammation) and what I was eating. Chapter 4 of his book *Stop Pain* should be required reading for anyone suffering back or joint pain. In fact, it should be a free handout from every doctor who has a patient with these and other chronic pain issues. He makes the connection between the standard American diet (SAD) and many of our medical ills. If chronic pain is one of your motivators for changing your eating habits, I strongly recommend you get this book and always have it nearby to reference.

Kathy Freston, *The Veganist*: One of my favorite TV shows is *Charlie Rose* on PBS. Quite by accident one night I was watching when this wonderful woman was a guest. I always was uncomfortable eating meat that had been raised in large factory/corporate farms because I knew those animals led horrible lives. But like other animal lovers, I continued to turn a blind eye when buying meat in a supermarket. No longer! She brought home to me that the contradiction was something I could no longer tolerate in my life. I went vegetarian for six months but have now come back around to being a "Flexitarian." (Chapter 10) I now only buy meat if I know how it was raised, and I eat relatively little of it.

Dr. William Davis, *Wheat Belly*, and **Melissa Diane Smith**, *Going Against the Grain*: I saw Dr. Davis on *The Dr. Oz Show* in December 2012. I remember the date because what he had to say was like a thunderbolt to me. Eating wheat, in all its forms, will make you fat and sick. This one simple concept significantly changed my food choices and health for good. There is more detail on this subject in "The Not So Good For You Foods" (Chapter 5).

Dr. Mark Hyman, *The Blood Sugar Solution*: This exceptionally accomplished, knowledgeable doctor and author is THE go-to guy for information on how food, in particular sugary, starchy food, leads to all sorts of health problems, one the most serious of which is diabetes. I believe he was the first to coin the term "diabesity" for a state of significant unhealthiness than occurs even without a formal diagnosis of diabetes. His work is a bit dense and complicated but extremely interesting and, yes, empowering. No wonder they chose him as "The Expert" to write the food part of the Daniel Plan book. I have learned a lot from him.

Mark Bittman, *VB6: Eat Vegan Before 6:00 to Lose Weight and Restore Your Health*. In addition to being an all-around great food writer, Mr. Bittman is a regular columnist for the *New York Times* and writes incredibly lucid articles about the convergence of food, big business, and politics.

Dr. Christiane Northrup: This wonderful woman and doctor who wrote *Women's Bodies, Women's Wisdom* in the '90s and has kept expertly writing on current challenges is my favorite expert in all things related to women's health.

And, of course, **Dr. Andrew Weil:** Dr. Weil gets a lot of credit in my book for being one of the pioneers in the health food movement. When he started talking about healthy eating in the '70s and '80s some folks thought he was really "out there." Now his work is adopted gospel in the mainstream. Of particular importance is his incredible expertise in the field of supplements. Whenever I am considering the wisdom of adding a supplement or vitamin, he is THE guy.

I would be remiss if I didn't mention all the information I received and the great debt I owe to both **PBS** and ***The Dr. Oz Show*** for bringing all these experts into my living room to make their cases to me in person. Dr. Oz has put brave, gutsy, and startlingly honest facts, experts, and ideas before the American people. Many times he will take a principled stand that goes against the mainstream of scientific, medical, or nutritional thought. Examples are issues surrounding wheat and gluten sensitivity, the problem of pesticides, labeling of GMOs, hidden junk/chemicals in processed food...the list goes on and on. It is because of him and the wide reach of his show that many Americans have stopped being robots dancing to the tunes of the Big Food Corporations and are thinking for themselves about health and nutrition. His website is a fountain of easy-to-access, easy-to-understand information on a full range of health topics. I know some folks think he goes off the rails with his promotion of exotic supplements and goofy demonstrations. But I don't mind those things and say - Keep up the good work, Dr. Oz!

19
This Is Nowhere
Near the End...

~~~~~~~~

Hopefully you have been working with the concepts in this book for about three to six months and there has been a change for the better in how you look and feel...CONGRATULATIONS!!!!

But I'm really hoping that whatever change has occurred leads you to explore more...to adapt your styles and tastes into your very own unique eating habits. Perhaps you want to explore Asian or Mexican food more. Or perhaps expand to some baking recipes with other flours besides wheat flour. Or maybe you just want to get better at gourmet healthy cooking in general. There are many really great books out there to help you do just that. Be careful to explore any book before purchase to make sure they don't rely on things you have worked so hard to get out of your life—i.e., "whole grain wheat" processed junk carbohydrates and artificial sweeteners.

The point is—you are now ready to tackle a whole new world of wonderful foods and great tastes.

Continued Good Luck and Good Health to You!

Diana Marshall

Author Biography

Diana Marshall is a first-time author who was inspired to write *No Pasta? Are You Kidding Me?!?* as a result of her own personal experiences of using food and simple cooking to battle her way back to better health.

At the peak of her career as an Appellate Administrative Law Judge, she was forced to retire after she suffered an attack of transverse myelitis, a severe neurological disorder. As she worked to manage her disabilities, she began a personal odyssey which took her to Mexico to live for three years. She then traveled around the United States with her welsh corgi Stanley looking for just the right place to settle. She eventually wound up in the Carolinas, living in Asheville and St. Helena's Island. A transplanted Californian, Diana now enjoys living in and exploring the natural beauty of the Southeast. You can follow her on Facebook or contact her directly at:

nopasta@outlook.com

Made in the USA
Lexington, KY
26 January 2015